The Three Mile Valley

Changing Our Conversations about Life and Loss

Dan Herod

Published in association with Books & Such Literary Management, www.booksandsuch.com

Cover by Hannah Linder Designs

ISBN-13: 979-8-218-15432-5 (pbk.) Herod, Dan, The three mile valley: changing conversations about life and loss /Dan Herod 1. Religion / Christian Church / General. 2. Religion / Christian Living / General

WHAT PEOPLE ARE SAYING

"Few have walked the road of suffering Dan has. The truth is we all will walk our own road, someday. Your details are different, but our pain is the same. That said, you will need a guide. Dan shows you the way through *The Three Mile Valley*. It's possible in your impossible. His life is the smoking gun to that truth." Eric Samuel Timm, Author and Speaker

"I've had the honor of knowing Dan for over a decade. Each time I hear his story it never fails to impact me. *The Three Mile Valley* is a compassion-filled book for every person walking through grief. Dan beautifully pairs empathy and applicable steps to journeying with Christ in the valley you are facing." Terrence Talley, Author and Speaker

"Dan's ability to draw from his own life experiences, the power of Scripture and insights of human psychology makes *The Three Mile Valley* a powerful book. He shares a message about walking through suffering, that our world and specifically the Church, desperately need. This book has changed my perspective on what it means to endure hardship as a follow of Jesus and how to help other in their journey towards wholeness." Pastor Nathan Schroeder

"*The Three Mile Valley* is an arrow of hope that hits a bull's eye in the gut of the broken-hearted. More than once, I caught myself looking up from the page to linger in the uniqueness of Dan's perspective. And his kind delivery of hard truths swept away lingering remnants of bitterness that have loitered too long in my own story." Janet Newberry, Author and Speaker

"If you or someone you love is walking through a valley of loss or suffering, the heart of this book will take you by the hand and lead you to the One who walks through valleys with you—Jesus. Every page of these chapters is dense with Biblical insight, hope, and strength for the valley-weary heart!" Cary Schmidt, Author and Pastor

"This book brings suffering out of the dark and into the light with a practical, Christ-centered path to lasting freedom. *The Three Mile Valley* is equipping and empowering as you walk through the pain of loss, setback, or disappointment. With transparency about his own journey, Dan Herod delivers hope and openness to areas that often leave us feeling stuck and isolated." Pastor Tom Murray

"*The Three Mile Valley* by Dan Herod paints a beautiful picture in the midst of our ruins and pain all while being a lighthouse, pointing to the only safe harbor we need, Jesus Christ." Amanda Hartwig, Bereavement Ministry Founder

"I've been the recipient of the well-meaning altruistic niceties that Dan addresses in *The Three Mile Valley*. This book is a true guide as you walk through pain, loss, death, and struggle. Jesus really is the Master Valley Walker, and this book shows you how He wants to walk through the valleys of suffering with you and help you come out on the other side experiencing abundant life." Pastor Preston Tippen

"Though all suffering is difficult, perhaps it is at its worst when we feel isolated and alone. *The Three Mile Valley* reads like a wise and close friend willing to run that path of suffering with you. Dan writes with kindness and transparency from his own reservoir of loss. Along the way, Dan will become not only a friend but will lead you to Christ, who also runs with you. So, take your time with this one and let it guide you through even the most challenging times, and let it lead you to hope." Chase Replogle, Author and Pastor

"*The Three Mile Valley* is not beautiful streams, flowing waterfalls, beautiful mountains sides, or amazing and abundant wildlife. It is a daunting journey through grief. Dan's personal insights will guide you through this journey." Dan Guarrero, Fire Department Chaplain and Pastor

"Dan invites you in—transparently and openly—as he and his family journey through one of the darkest challenges one could face. Dan shatters the silence with a fresh, positive, and biblical perspective." Kent Hulbert, National Youth Alive Missionary

Dedication

To all who have walked or are walking
The Three Mile Valley,
longing for someone to whisper
"This is not synonymous with Forever."

You can make it.
Keep breathing.
Always choose the better way.
Your story is not done yet.

CONTENTS

Have you ever felt like you were running a race
you didn't sign up for?
You don't want to be there, but you
can't be anywhere else.

CHAPTER ONE

Life

My lungs burned. The crisp autumn air ignited my heaving chest as it begged for oxygen. I began to wonder: *Will this race ever end*?

When I was in high school, I ran cross country for one season. Why on God's green earth did I sign up for a sport like that? Running is hard! If you do it right, all you want to do is stop.

Your heart pounds and your whole-body cries tears of pain. Most people call this sweating. When I run, my body does not sweat. It sobs tears of regret.

If you're lucky, the beads of sweat will miss your eyes as they travel down your forehead and off the tip of your nose. Every time I go for a jog, the salty rivers flow directly into the inside corner of both eyes.

While suffering does not necessarily mean you are running, running most certainly means you are suffering to some degree.

It wasn't all bad, though. One of my favorite races was in Duluth, Minnesota. It was called the Swain Cross Country Invitational. Swain has been running every fall since 1951. This race boasts a challenging three-mile course and draws teams from all over the region.

I will never forget when my cross-country team approached the outskirts of Duluth on our coach bus. While my face wasn't necessarily pressed up against the window next to my seat, I was struck by the intense beauty that welcomed me to town.

The picturesque scene rolled up and down endless hills surrounding the city. Beautiful browns, yellows, and greens fused into a masterpiece collage that took my breath away.

The large coach bus came to a clean stop at the racecourse, and my teammates and I exited with great anticipation.

We completed our pre-race preparations and headed to the starting line. It was time to do what we'd come to do.

At the starting line before the race began, with runners to my right and left, I looked up. Towering before me was the hill we would climb. Yes, you read that right. This race started in a valley. Imagine running across a soccer field that tilted up. Going down would be easy. Running up it would be a grind.

With one crisp blast, the starting gun filled the valley. The sound of my shoes pounding the grass adding to the deafening rumble created by the crush of runners. My ascent out of the valley had begun.

The hill beckoned me at the start of the race. It menaced me again in the middle. Taunting me one last time, it held my finish line.

Ascending out of the valley three times made one thing clear; this was one hill of a race! I had to overcome this valley in all three miles of this contest.

Each time I approached the valley, a sense of dread filled me. I knew the difficulty ahead. Running out of the valley was physically, mentally, and emotionally exhausting.

Everything in me wanted to collapse in defeat.

Discouragement hit me hard as I raced out of the valley the second time. Legs aching, and lungs burning, my arms felt like sandbags attached to my shoulders. This body of mine desperately wanted me to quit my race every time I entered the valley.

Despite feeling I couldn't possibly go on, I finished the race. This brings me to the first lesson of conquering every valley in life:

It is only when we refuse to give up
that we cross finish lines.

Life can be a lot like my cross-country race in Duluth. Some stretches are so beautiful that they take your breath away. Other parts are so difficult you can barely breathe.

When you experience a valley, or a hard time in life, it can become a season of suffering that begs you to despair—to lose hope. We will all find ourselves smack dab in the middle of a valley eventually.

How we walk through a moment like this changes everything. When we choose a hope-filled perspective, we become powerful.

Even as we endure the worst that life throws at us, we can discover just how strong God has designed us to be. Yes, that divorce may have stunned you, and left you struggling to catch your breath. In that moment, you didn't think you could ever move forward and live a great life.

No matter what has thrown you into a valley in life, it does not have enough potency to stop you permanently. Losing your loved one long before you were ready to let them go may have silenced your song for a night.

God has an answer in your pain that will fill you with joy again.

Your race is real, and God wants you to win. How you run through every season—easy or hard, comfortable or difficult—is important. The way you navigate the *valleys* of life has a profound impact. How you journey through difficult seasons will shape your life for years to come.

I believe it is time to change the way we talk about the valleys in life. The reason why is because we have become too comfortable simplifying suffering. You have probably heard one of the following statements.

1.) "God would never give you more than you can handle."
2.) "Everything happens for a reason."
3.) "Time heals everything."

What if these three sentences are doing more harm than good?

In 2011 Barbara Oakley, PhD and Guruprasad Madhaven released a book called *Pathological Altruism.* They argue that sometimes our attempts to help someone hurts them. Our actions make us feel better, but they don't help the one in pain get better.

When good intentions go awry, we have what exists today. Well-intentioned words unintentionally wounding those already afflicted by life.

It doesn't have to be this way. We can change the conversations we have about life and loss. The words we use to describe the most painful moments in life can draw people closer to God, not drive them away from Him. Thoughts we share can comfort and heal those walking through the valley of life. This includes you and me too.

When someone runs a marathon, water stations are sprinkled throughout the course. Wouldn't it be crazy if the staff working those tables handed out little cards with encouraging slogans instead of water?

I fear we have done this far too long. As people run for their lives, we dispense clichés and catchphrases. Good intentions, gone awry.

People in pain need to be refreshed more than they need a pep talk.

Life is a race full of struggle, hard decisions, and sacrifice. To finish, you must keep running. If you can't run, walk. If you can't walk, crawl.

You can learn how to persevere when everything inside of you wants to quit.

When you identify the lies and half-truths that have bound up so many people, you are on the right track.

God intentionally uses the metaphor of running to help us understand how He sees life. Read the following verses from the book of Hebrews:

> *Therefore, since we are surrounded by such a great cloud of witnesses, let us throw off everything that hinders and the sin that so easily entangles. And let us run with perseverance the race marked out for us, fixing our eyes on Jesus, the pioneer and perfecter of faith. For the joy set before him he endured the cross, scorning its shame, and sat down at the right hand of the throne of God. — Hebrews 12:1–2 (NIV)*

You may not always be conscious of it, but every step you take is echoed by the One who runs beside you. He is with you. You're not alone.

You are also surrounded by the entire family of faith. They watch you now from heaven and here on earth. Everyone wants you to finish.

Painful valleys can make or break you. These seasons of suffering remind us that life is not fair. Longing for relief from the agony is normal. Leveraging your discomfort for your own good is not.

Every aching inch of The Three Mile Valley is an opportunity to transform into someone stronger, wiser, and more compassionate. When you see this moment as a cocoon, rather than a tomb, you set the stage for true metamorphosis.

What we do when we are down and out has power. This potential is full of hope for every single one of us.

You may be in a valley right now where the difficulty you face is more than you can handle. A friend of yours may need you to walk through their painful valley with them.

It may be that you are watching someone journey through their valley from a distance. Regardless of where you find yourself right now, you can equip your soul with the tools you need to overcome life's most challenging times.

Seasons of suffering bring you to your knees in agony. Even then, you have a say in how the story unfolds.

How we choose to navigate dark days and long, lonely nights holds the key to a better life.

The intensity of the valley in the Swain race is a continual reminder to me that in this life we will encounter suffering. We will experience our own variation of "The Three Mile Valley"—a metaphorical place intended to represent our literal path through life's darkest days.

The race was over three miles long, with each mile different than the others because of its terrain. Although it felt more like a test, it was my classroom.

The trail was my teacher, and I was the student.

Terrain transformed into an instructor that unpacked key lessons I will carry for the rest of my life. As I persevered through that cross-country race, I encountered the following truth:

What you believe about God and yourself has
the power to keep you from the finish line,
or push you far past it.

It's time to move away from Christian-sounding clichés like "God would never give you more than you can handle" and towards biblical truth that offers hope.

Drop the damaging declaration "Everything happens for a reason" and pick up the hope-filled truth Scripture reveals.

Jettison the empty "Time heals everything" and load up on the empowering, healing wisdom found in God's Word.

Watch "Running is Dumb"
at HopeBetweenTheLines.com

CONVERSATION STARTERS

Chapter One Questions

Question: Do you agree with the author that it is time to change the conversation about life and loss? Why or why not?

____

____

____

____

____

____

____

Question: What are some other things people have said to you as you go through a valley in life? What helped? What didn't?

____

____

____

____

____

____

____

Action: Identify a tough stretch you have gone through in the past and reflect on how other people's words impacted you.

____

____

____

____

____

____

"The world breaks everyone and, afterward,
many are strong in broken places."

Ernest Hemingway

CHAPTER TWO

The Three Mile Valley

The Concept

The Three Mile Valley represents the deepest, darkest moments of life. This is where you experience a soul-scorching pain that changes the essence of who you are.

You find yourself here after you lose a loved one. A devastating disappointment can transport you into this realm of shadows. Debilitating depression plunges you into the lonely, cavernous depths of this forsaken place.

Suffering from a chronic illness reroutes your life through this valley.

This unforgiving environment pulls you deeper into the ache of your agony and sucks the life out of you. It is merciless and unrelenting. This is no ordinary three-mile trek.

Don't envision a literal three miles, three days, or three years. Picture endless desert stretching to the horizon. A path that descends into perilous, jagged perches that demand you choose every step wisely. A slip here can cost you dearly.

The climb out reveals an end that promises to be different, but possibly better. This is The Three Mile Valley. A place where you and I discover the truth about ourselves, others, and God.

Here, in The Three Mile Valley, we are reminded that what we say matters. Words to ourselves, to others, and to God all propel our story down a track that will carry us somewhere, eventually.

It is possible to take stock of the words on the shelves of our minds.

There is no better time than now to inventory the thoughts we embrace, because they ultimately become our truth. Not The Truth, but the temporary perspective we all have.

This take on life sets the stage for our story that will either unfold into something beautiful or unravel into deep despair.

Everyone walks through The Three Mile Valley eventually. Like standing in a torrential downpour, you know you're in the middle of one because everything is soaking wet.

As the wind whips all around you, every single story you've heard your parents tell you of the storms they've weathered suddenly come to life.

One of those days happened to my family on July 20th, 2019.

We were enjoying a lazy summer Saturday when a weather alert lit up my cell phone. The text message from the national weather service said **SEVERE THUNDERSTORM WARNING.**

We've been through storms like that before. I wasn't worried. Minutes later, the next alert came through. **TORNADO WARNING. TAKE SHELTER NOW.**

Marlena and the kids all sprang into action to find refuge in our basement. I carried our golden retriever, Bailey, down the stairs to safety. She does not do storms well at all.

Sirens blared in the distance. Fierce rain pelted our house.

Suddenly, a blast of wind tore down our street, snapping trees like toothpicks. Booming, deep cracks thundered as timber splintered in every direction.

A large limb from the ancient silver maple tree outside our house tore off and came crashing down mere inches from the window next to our living room. It wrenched the powerline right out of our siding.

Sparks sprayed vivid white like it was the Fourth of July.

As we all huddled in our makeshift shelter, all we could do was wait for the storm to pass.

It left as fast as it arrived.

After several minutes of calm, we emerged from the basement to survey the damage. Thankfully, there wasn't one reported injury in our entire area. This is incredible when you consider that a burst of straight-line winds nailed the local campground, full of families in tents and campers.

Every description I have ever heard or read pales in comparison to what we experienced that day. Even the movies that I've seen couldn't compete.

The thunder from our storm was felt in the bones. Lighting emblazoned on the back of the brain. Wind seemed to touch the center of the soul. It was as real as real can get.

Walking through The Three Mile Valley is like surviving a powerful, relentless storm. A painful valley becomes all too real when you're in it. Every description you've heard from others seems inadequate when hardship visits your home. When it passes, you're left to pick up the pieces.

Somehow, you must find a way forward.

My Three Mile Valley

On November 30, 2011, my family stepped into the darkest, most shadowy, incomprehensible valley we have ever encountered.

We still walk this valley.

The details of that fateful day that started it all are still fresh in my mind.

None of us had any clue a storm was racing toward us from just over the horizon. It wasn't an actual weather pattern with clouds, wind, rain, and thunder. It was much, much worse.

As dawn approached, everyone was fast asleep, and silence filled the air.

The rudeness of my alarm clock pulled me out of slumber. With a groan, I forced myself out of bed to begin my day. I walked out of our bedroom and turned left into my daughter's room. Peyton was already standing in her crib, ready to greet the day.

Her thirteen-month-old gibberish was sounding more and more like English every day. By now she had mastered the most important word in the English language: "Da-da."

Those syllables echoed off the walls of her room and landed straight in my heart that morning. Like every dad, I loved hearing her say my name.

Her eyes lit up as I reached to pick her up.

We enjoyed a simple breakfast, as we did most mornings. Peyton loved sharing a banana with me as I took in the peace before my busy day.

When it was time for me to head to the office, I transferred parental control to my bride and drove into work.

Marlena called mid-morning with an update on Peyton's doctor visit, a routine check-up for a one-year-old.

A smile stretched across my face as she informed me that the pediatrician said Peyton was perfect.

We already knew that.

With our daughter's clean bill of health in hand, Marlena carried on with the rest of her day. What was the plan? A brief lunch stop, and then a lengthy nap for our perfect princess.

Peyton was our miracle baby. After our son, Logan, was born, we endured back-to-back miscarriages. Two heartbreaks in a row were too much to handle.

When we found out that Marlena was pregnant a fourth time, we were cautiously optimistic.

Cautious optimism transformed into confident optimism as Marlena entered the second trimester.

Confident optimism became complete joy as we welcomed Peyton Elizabeth Herod into the world on October 23, 2010. She represented life after two heartbreaking deaths.

My heart soared that day and every day after Peyton arrived. She was perfect, and the visit to the pediatrician's office had just reminded us of that.

After Marlena finished giving me the update over the phone, she went home to lay our daughter down for a nap.

I dove right back into my work at the office.

When I arrived home later that afternoon, Peyton was still napping. I hugged my son Logan and then grabbed a spot on the floor beside him in front of our living room TV.

At a few minutes before five, I squeezed Logan one last time and kissed Marlena goodbye. I got in my car and headed off to speak to students at a youth ministry meeting.

Less than five minutes after leaving, I got the phone call that changed my life forever.

It was Marlena.

I answered the way I do every time she calls: "Hey Cutie."

She never acknowledged my greeting. What she said next hit me like a tsunami.

The panic in her voice let me know something was terribly wrong. She described every parent's worst nightmare in a few short words and ended the phone call by saying, "Come home now!"

She hung up to call 911.

My heart raced furiously. I slammed on the brakes and made a U-turn in the middle of the road.

My mind spun like a washing machine in its final spin cycle as I replayed Marlena's words. Had I heard her right? How was that possible?

I sped home and broke several laws along the way. The car screeched to a halt in the driveway. I sprinted into the garage, through the kitchen, and down the hall toward Peyton's room.

I was greeted by a sight I can't erase from my mind.

My beautiful baby girl lay lifeless on the floor.

This was far worse than any nightmare. She hadn't been breathing for a while. I fell to my knees, struggling to understand what was happening.

Marlena administered CPR as I watched in horror. Peyton's chest rose and fell with every breath her loving momma exhaled into her. I was helpless as a husband and father.

I did the only thing I could think to do and laid my hand on Peyton's chest. With all the faith I had, I cried in a whisper, "Jesus, please!"

After uttering my two-word prayer, I realized our four-year-old Logan was standing just outside Peyton's bedroom.

I grabbed him by the hand to sit on the couch in our living room. As we walked down the hallway, first responders began to arrive.

The house bloated with intense activity as more first responders arrived. A sheriff, EMTs, and paramedics—a concert of trained professionals all worked intensely to bring our little girl back to life.

Our princess was loaded in the back of an ambulance. But I think I already knew the futility of that trip.

The decision was made on the way to the hospital to halt all life-saving attempts.

Peyton had passed.

That evening, we sat in a hospital room holding our baby girl's body in our arms, stunned by the reality that she was no longer with us. Shattered and shocked, we struggled to grasp how heaven gained what we had so tragically lost.

Friends and family began to arrive after they heard Peyton had been rushed to the hospital. The emergency room waiting area filled now with our loved ones who still did not know the rest of the story.

Someone needed to tell them.

When I faced them, I could sense they knew the news was not good. All I could say was, "She's gone."

We found out later that our beautiful baby girl had been taken by sudden infant death syndrome (SIDS).

Ever since that fateful evening, we have spent countless hours immersed in grief and covered in tears.

Years have passed now since we lost our Peyton, and yet I am still awash in the intense agony of that tragic night.

I wonder what Peyton would look like today. I'm confident she would be beautiful like her momma. And just a little sassy, also like her momma.

Walking through The Three Mile Valley is emotionally crippling. It is like being slowly crushed by a massive iceberg. As you flail against uninvited devastation, it dominates your field of view. You can't *not* see it. Everywhere you look, you see the very thing that is crashing into you.

For me and my family, it was this moment in time that felt like eternity was unraveling from the inside out.

For you, it may be the cancer that slammed into your life. Shards of your deepest hopes and dreams splinter into a million pieces as they spray in every direction.

Sending the core temperature of your soul sub-zero, this freezing loss mercilessly squeezes the life from you.

You can't *not* feel it.

That is, until you go numb.

I have grown to see this journey as a walk through the metaphorical Three Mile Valley.

While it will not last forever, we will walk through it for the rest of our lives.

CONVERSATION STARTERS

Chapter Two Questions

Question: In what ways do you see our culture expecting Jesus to provide an easy life? In what ways have you personally fallen into this way of thinking?

____

____

____

____

____

____

____

____

____

Question: The author describes the personal tragedy that shaped his view of suffering and began his walk through The Three Mile Valley. Take a moment to journal or share a past or current life event that created ongoing suffering in your life.

____

____

____

____

____

____

____

____

Action: Identify someone in your life who is going through a season of suffering (even if you are as well). Commit to praying for that person regularly. Ask God to reveal other ways you can reach out and share His comforting presence with them.

Sometimes you choose the path.
Sometimes the path chooses you.

CHAPTER THREE

The Four Paths

While all of us will suffer, we will not all suffer the same way. I lost my daughter tragically and suddenly. You may have lost your health or your job.

Maybe you are battling extreme depression or estrangement from a loved one.

Just because our losses are different doesn't diminish one or the other. Walking through a season of suffering is hard no matter the details.

The Three Mile Valley has four distinct pathways through it. Observe the four ways life may bring us to and through suffering.

The Temporary Path

The temporary path is a common one we take through The Three Mile Valley. There is a very good chance that you have already walked it. Most people will take multiple journeys through The Three Mile Valley on this trail.

This temporary season of suffering can last anywhere from a few weeks to many months.

Just because it is a temporary season does not mean it is easy. These temporary seasons can be intense and overwhelming. They can include challenging circumstances like:

- Job loss
- Short-term illnesses
- Unfulfilled expectations
- Discouragement
- Disappointment
- Unanswered prayer for a family member making unwise decisions

How we walk through temporary challenges is important because it affects us down the road. The way you suffer temporarily shapes how you suffer permanently.

Why? The power of precedent. Habits we cultivate, for better or for worse, walk with us into the future.

When I was nineteen years old, I was called to jury duty. It was a truly fascinating experience I will never forget.

The court case involved a man, alcohol, and a firearm. Throughout the trial, we heard multiple testimonies and examined a lot of evidence. It was our job, as the jury, to determine whether the man was guilty.

After much deliberation, we the jury found him guilty, because there was sufficient evidence to convict him.

We found out later that this man had a history of breaking the law. What he did before influenced what he did next.

In other words, he planted the seed of a bad habit the first time he broke the law. Instead of changing his behavior and ripping out the root, he allowed the seed to become a weed.

Over time, his bad habit overtook him. One bad step led to a second. Two poor choices multiplied many times over, and the tiny root bore painful fruit for him and his loved ones.

How does his story apply to your temporary path in The Three Mile Valley? You owe it to yourself to choose wisely through these temporary seasons because they influence your future suffering.

Don't let the name of the path fool you into thinking that it is any less powerful or important. When you endure short-term setbacks with wisdom, you equip yourself with better emotional and spiritual health that you get to take with you when you leave this valley.

Should you find yourself in The Three Mile Valley again, all the good seeds (wise choices) travel with you and become more automatic.

This is not a promise of future perfection. Rather, it is the power of repetition on full display for us.

How different will your present be when you choose what is better today because you want a stronger tomorrow?

The Sustained Path

The sustained path feels like it will never end. This adds extra weight to our already heavy burden. *How much longer will I have to do this?* is the question that gnaws away at our strength in The Three Mile Valley.

Chipping away at our resolve, this added challenge often wears us down and saps our will to get back up should we trip and fall.

Every sustained path through The Three Mile Valley has a defined beginning. However, there is no way to know when it will end. The challenges common on this specific path include:

- Significant relational strife
- Chronic illness
- Financial hardships
- Professional setbacks
- A wayward teen or adult child makes life-altering mistakes with long-lasting effects

When you walk the sustained path, you have the power to change your future for the better. You can avoid the pitfall of authoring additional hardship for yourself.

This is easier said than done, though. When you can't see the finish line, it's easy to lose sight of what is worth fighting for.

The truth is that *you're* worth fighting for. You owe it to yourself to steward this season of suffering well. Because it is possible to choose wisely while you suffer.

When you walk this path with wisdom, you won't let the unknown timeline undo all the good things you still have in your life.

You can avoid the self-sabotage that is oh so easy to fall into.

The Secret Path

The secret path is lonely. Even when you're in the middle of a crowded room, you feel disconnected from everyone and everything. No one knows you're hurting. You've done a great job covering up the wounds you're nursing in solitude.

The addiction you're ashamed of is one of your best kept secrets. Past trauma that hasn't been shared with a trusted person haunts you from the shadows. Your high functioning depression has everyone convinced that you are doing great. If they only knew how you are *really doing.*

Like prison bars on a cell, the solitude of your suffering adds additional layers of pain. Even if your loved ones know about your struggle, you can't seem to shake the feeling that no one cares. You know you are walking the secret path when your circumstance includes:

- Addiction
- Depression
- Unrevealed abuse
- Severe regret

A recent survey estimated that 21.5 million Americans meet the criteria for substance use disorder (SUDS).[1] Roughly 8 percent of people ages twelve and older are addicted to alcohol or illicit drugs.

The sobering truth is that this statistic is more than a number to many reading this book right now. You have a friend, family member, or coworker who is battling addiction, and it's breaking your heart.

Or you might be the one battling an addiction and are in a fight for your very life.

Your secret path might be a recent wound, dangerous habit, secret sin, or emotional trauma that remains unrevealed to this day.

You owe it to yourself to invite others into your story. People who are ready and able to help you walk your path.

Your healing will be a journey that requires wise, caring, and trustworthy voices that speak truth to your weary soul. Compassionate souls that listen to you and are comfortable with the silence when you can't find the words.

When we learn to navigate this path with others, we find our footing a little more secure.

The Tragic Path

The tragic path is marked by the loss of a loved one. Like losing an arm, the loss of someone you never wanted to live without has not ended your own life, but it has undeniably changed it.

This suffering is found in the presence of your loved one's absence.

It is the agonizing awareness that they are gone.

The goodness, joy, laughter, and sense of belonging their presence created has left with them.

Learning to live without someone you love is just plain hard. How do you live a life you don't want?

Grief forces you to face a painful reality you are struggling to understand. Over time, you can learn to accept it, but it never feels fully right. It almost seems insulting to their memory to move forward without them.

I know now that moving forward is one of the most powerful ways to *honor* them, because you *carry* their memory with you for the rest of your life. Every single smile, laugh, tear and warm hug you shared with them is yours to cherish.

If you are walking the tragic path, I am deeply sorry for your loss.

You owe it to yourself to carry your suffering well on this path for two reasons. 1) The life you still have is worth living, even if you don't feel that way right now. 2) Choosing wisely honors the one you lost, because it gives you the opportunity to keep their memory alive as you carry it forward with you, but in a way that strengthens rather than destroys you.

No one ever sets up a campsite in the middle of a path because paths are there to help find your way to your desired destination.

These four routes through The Three Mile valley are all different from one another. Each one has different characteristics and challenges. However, one uniting fact exists for them all: They aren't intended to be a place you stay indefinitely.

Our hope in every valley is that we are on the way through to the other side.

Watch "The Four Paths"
at HopeBetweenTheLines.com

CONVERSATION STARTERS

Chapter Three Questions

Question: Would you describe your current suffering as temporary, sustained, secret, or tragic? Which of these paths have you already experienced?

Question: When have you experienced a merging of two paths? How has this interaction of paths affected your journey through the season of suffering?

____

____

____

____

____

____

____

____

Action: Journal about your current suffering. Take special note of how God is showing you His grace one day at a time as you walk through The Three Mile Valley.

"Jesus made the extreme sacrifice
on Good Friday. And he went to
the edge of the ledge on Holy Saturday,
into death and darkness itself.
On Easter Sunday
he blew the world wide open,
exploding into birth a new creation,
commissioning his disciples to follow him
out to the edges of creation."

Leonard Sweet

CHAPTER FOUR

The Master Valley Walker

Moving forward through The Three Mile Valley is easier said than done. Disappointment and despair mess with your mind as you try to make sense of it all. One question we all wrestle with is *How do I get through this?* The answer to that question is as much about *who you walk with* as is it about *how* you walk.

The company we keep will either help us cross the finish line or hinder us from ever reaching it. You need to choose to walk with someone who knows their way through and has the power to help finish the journey.

There will be obstacles that are bigger and stronger than you. Grief, traumatic experiences, and depression are three giants that require us to call for backup.

Your friends and family are God-given. Keep them close as you tread through the darkest valleys.

There is one more person you need to have right by your side as you walk.

Jesus Is the Master Valley Walker

When you're eyeball-deep in a sea of suffering, it feels like you are going under. Who do you turn to when you're facing something bigger than you?

Where will you find strength when life is a valley, not a mountain top?

You need someone who knows the terrain better than you do. The Master Valley Walker.

Regardless of the specific path you are on, He is someone greater who has already gone before you. This encouraging reality is unpacked in the Bible.

Hebrews 4:15 says "For we do not have a high priest who is unable to empathize with our weaknesses, but we have one who has been tempted in every way, just as we are – yet he did not sin" (NIV).

It's been said that people are *attracted* to your strengths and beauty but *connect* to you through your weaknesses. Jesus was so compelled to help us in our predicament that He couldn't stay away.

Through our value in Him, He connects with us through weakness.

He experienced what life is like for you and me and felt everything you and I feel. Jesus was tempted (Luke 4:1-14). At the end of His earthly life, He was betrayed (Luke 22:47-48). Enduring indescribable pain, He experienced psychological torture and physical injury (Mark 15:16-20).

The scriptures label Jesus as a man of sorrows, acquainted with grief (Isaiah 53:3).

Jesus felt it all and empathizes with us in our situation. He became like us in the truest sense and maintained His divine nature.

In one of his brilliant lectures when I was at North Central University (Minneapolis, MN), Dr. Amos Yong said that Jesus is the most *human* being there ever was. The reason is that He stayed close to our Heavenly Father while He was on earth, experiencing a realm of life that God originally intended for all of us.

Because Jesus did it right, we have hope.

Jesus' impact didn't end with His feeling everything we feel. He took it all the way through a supernatural resurrection.

This frames up a powerful truth that changes everything for you and me.

In John 16:33 (NLT), Jesus declares:

> *I have told you all this so that you may have peace in me. Here on earth you will have many trials and sorrows. But take heart, because I have overcome the world.*

When I hear bad news or a negative report, I want it to come layered in optimism. I love the way Jesus tells it like it is. He pulls no punches and tells us how life is going to go.

Let's look at the first layer of John 16:33.

Jesus promises us peace in Him. When you're suffering, peace is power, because it calms the storm inside of you. His presence in your valley changes you but doesn't guarantee your situation will change.

Following Jesus doesn't exempt us from hard times. We are going to feel pain in life, with or without Jesus.

When Jesus is the name you trust more, you receive more than you could ever pay for. His presence changes everything because He is greater than the obstacle you can't overcome.

His presence promises peace as your problems promise pain. Your pain is powerful, but Jesus is powerful too.

Peace is not the absence of opposition.
It is the presence of Someone greater.

Jesus gave us the good news, and now it is time for some bad news.

According to Him, we will have "many trials and sorrows." Multiple. More than one.

It should come as no surprise that some stretches of life will break us down. The exact word Jesus chose to use means *tribulation*, which is another way to say "Ouchie mama!"

Now for more good news. Jesus has conquered every sickness, setback, dysfunction, and disease we will ever encounter. He didn't just battle on our behalf. He overcame in our place. This makes Him the Master Valley Walker.

Jesus conquered your darkest day and your loneliest night as He hung on the cross. You don't have to suffer in solitude because your valley has the footprints of Jesus all over it.

I love the fact that because He suffered in our place, we can have peace in every place we suffer.

What does this mean for you?

Jesus walked The Three Mile Valley. He overcame everything that overcomes you. There is nothing too hard for Him. He is the way forward, your newfound sense of hope.

Now, He walks beside you in life. The 23rd Psalm reminds us that He is the good shepherd who walks with us *through* the valley of the shadow of death.

This brings us to the first cliché we've all heard too many times: God would never give you more than you can handle. This most definitely is not true.

You can attest to seasons in your own life when you were stretched past your limits. I personally know what it is like to be so depressed that I would have been okay if I stopped existing.

The powerful truth we can all embrace in place of the catchphrase above is this: God would never give you more than *He* can handle.

This simple, yet profound truth changes everything. You don't have to have all the answers because God does.

We don't have to keep it all together, because our Creator is holding us in the palm of His hand.

When we are weak, He is strong (2 Corinthians 12:9).

Watch "The Master Valley Walker"
at HopeBetweenTheLines.com

CONVERSATION STARTERS

Chapter Four Questions

Question: Sometimes we try to find strength apart from the Lord. What are some common places people look for comfort and peace when they are in a valley? Where do you seek strength and peace in difficulty?

____

____

____

____

____

____

____

Question: How do you respond to the inevitability of suffering? Does that reality fill you with fear, anger, or frenzy? How can you look to the future with hope and peace?

____

____

____

____

____

____

____

____

Action: What are tangible reminders that help you realize God's presence in your pain? Music, art, scriptures, and creation can all speak to us of God's heart and character as we walk through our darkest valley. Choose one of these reminders that has meant a lot to you and share it with the suffering friend for whom you are praying.

“Standing in the kingdom, we make
responsible decisions in love, with
assurance that how things turn out for us
does not really matter that much because,
in any case, we *are* in the kingdom
of the heavens. In that kingdom
nothing that can happen to us
is ‘the end of the world.’”

Dallas Willard

CHAPTER FIVE

The First Mile: Now Is Not Forever

Mile one of The Three Mile Valley is distinctively flat. Blistering heat scorches your soul mercilessly, as waves of anger and doubt sweep over you.

It looks like it goes on forever.

Barren and lifeless, discouragement is the bedrock under every step.

This is where we learn to think better, so we can get better.

We Are All Pathological

When you look in the mirror, what do you see and what do you say? The answer to both those questions matter more than you might think.

Pastor and author Paul David Tripp highlights the power you possess between your ears when he says, "No one is more influential in your life than you are, because no one talks to you more than you do."[2]

God has given us the ability to shape the way we see ourselves in our world.

As you journey through The Three Mile Valley, your thoughts will take you down a predictable path.

This trail is the result of a million meditations.

I'm talking about the simple statements you tell yourself over and over that become the guardrails that frame your thought process into a familiar pattern.

Silent declarations like, *I am enough* or *This will all work out in the end.*

When you repeatedly tell yourself this truth, a powerful Path of Logic is forming deep within you.

This is great news if you're telling yourself the truth. What happens if you aren't, though?

If half-truths and deceptions delivered from the enemy of your soul shape the conversations you have with yourself, your Path of Logic is compromised. A lie repeated often enough sounds an awful lot like the truth. *I'm not enough. Nothing good ever comes my way.*

These damaging declarations don't come from the heart of your loving Creator, but from the dark depths of your eternal enemy.

The Three Mile Valley is where you discover your Paths of Logic. If it is time to change your mind, God is ready to help you get healthier in the best possible way.

A helpful nudge to stay on the right train of thought is at your fingertips. God's written word, The Bible. It is true illumination for key decisions. A warm, comforting light to aid in your trek, a lantern for your path (Psalm 119:105).

The scriptures are also powerful, like a sword. They cut through every layer of thought and get straight to the heart (Hebrews 4:12).

When the word of God is brought into the deepest part of who we are, it accurately judges what we believe. It is in this moment that God shows us just how powerful He is.

While you and I can assess the outward look a person has, God sees straight through our external layers of makeup and isn't fooled by the ways we cover up (1

Samuel 16:7). He knows our hearts better than we do, and in a spiritual sense, He can heal every wounded chamber.

The tools God provides can help you forge a true and healthy Path of Logic as you walk through darkest valleys.

A light and a sword.

And amazingly, both are found within the pages of the Holy Scriptures.

Leverage this illumination for your benefit and see more clearly than before. Handle this weapon for your soul's protection, cutting down lies to stop them dead in their tracks.

Walking with Jesus, the Master Valley Walker, is only possible when you keep the Bible close.

As the heat of unrelenting agony scorches your soul, it will feel impossible to take another step sometimes.

The *now* you face will seem like *forever*. You will probably wonder *Will this ever end?*

The Bible has good news for you. The valley is temporary. All of it.

Now Is Not Forever—Think Better

Your three-mile trial cannot last forever. God has imposed limits on every season. Note the wording of Ecclesiastes chapter 3.

> *For everything there is a season, a time for every activity under heaven.*
> *A time to be born and a time to die.*
> *A time to plant and a time to harvest.*
> *A time to kill and a time to heal.*
> *A time to tear down and a time to build up.*
> *A time to cry and a time to laugh.*
> *A time to grieve and a time to dance.*
> *A time to scatter stones and a time to gather stones.*
> *A time to embrace and a time to turn away.*
> *A time to search and a time to quit searching.*
> *A time to keep and a time to throw away.*
> *A time to tear and a time to mend.*
> *A time to be quiet and a time to speak.*
> *A time to love and a time to hate. A time for war and a time for peace.*
> *— Ecclesiastes 3:1–8 (NLT)*

Verse 4 is especially beautiful: "A time to cry and a time to laugh. A time to grieve and a time to dance."

Time—with boundaries.

God reminds us that although we cry, we will not cry forever. The sounds of our sorrow will be replaced by joyful laughter. Our grief will be replaced with dancing. The pit of despair will be filled with vibrant celebration. Someday.

Every season of suffering has an expiration date. Keeping this in focus doesn't diminish the difficulty you face or lessen the pain. What it does accomplish for you will stay with you all the way through The Three Mile Valley, because this is a helpful Path of Logic.

The valley is not your home, your destination. God will give this place a powerful purpose. It will be good for you in the end.

Meditate on this regularly and cultivate healthier thought patterns. It will help you experience an incredible personal transformation.

Renovation Station

My in-laws asked me to help with a large renovation project at their house. Their kitchen and dining room needed an upgrade. We couldn't just nail new drywall over the old and slap a fresh coat of paint on it. The plan called for radical changes that would enhance the function, flow, and feel of the entire first floor.

Electrical wiring was going to be ripped out and replaced. Plumbing would be rerouted. An entire wall was going "bye-bye." The old had to go to make room for the new.

Equipped with an array of tools of all kinds, our spartan crew began the demolition phase. A section of ceiling came crashing down with a thunderous clatter that was felt by everyone in the house. I thought to myself, *Boy, I am glad I wasn't under that when it gave way!*

Walls disintegrated into chunks of drywall and fine powder.

Percussive thuds punctuated the din of vibrant and violent activity.

Cabinets and countertops didn't stand a chance against the army of sledgehammers deployed that day.

By the end of the day, the kitchen sink found itself out of a job as it lay in the dumpster, covered in shards of debris.

The demolition process was occasionally chaotic. The volume was so intense at times that we would have to shout, or resort to speaking between strikes of the sledgehammer. However, this doesn't mean it was aimless or careless.

My father-in-law made sure everything we did fit the end goal.

The work would come to a full stop whenever there was question about how much of the old had to go. We could not afford to remove anything that supported the overall structure of the house. Removing a load-bearing wall would be catastrophic.

A mistake like that would threaten the stability of the entire house. Compromising the foundation would imperil everything and everyone inside.

Your soul is like a house, and your beliefs and values map out the rooms. You will have ample opportunity to renovate your life as you walk through The Three Mile Valley. The storms that come will reveal where you've got a leaky seal. Seasons of life will lead you to realign whole areas that are no longer functional.

Whatever you choose to do through your seasons of suffering, I encourage you to build your life on the words of Jesus Christ.

Demolition is part of renovation that leads to genuine renewal.

My in-laws' house is much better now than it was before. Appliances smartly placed line the perimeter of a fully functional kitchen. Generous natural lighting pours through skylights and floods the room with warmth. The beautiful open concept flows into a spacious dining room as authentic relationship flourishes over delicious meals.

Many dollars spent and countless drops of sweat made it happen, because transformation has a price tag.

When we want to upgrade our lives, we must release what was. There may be a path of logic in your life that needs to be demolished. Three lies I've identified that need to go are 1) God would never give you more than you can handle, 2) Everything happens for a reason, 3) Time heals everything. Beyond these suffocating thought patterns are many more.

"I am unlovable."
"Bad things always happen to me, good things always happen to everyone else."
"God must really hate me."

As it relates to the way we think, God wants to give us a healthier way.

Read the following verse and focus on the second half.

> *We demolish arguments and every pretension that sets itself up against the knowledge of God, and we take captive every thought to make it obedient to Christ.* — 2 Corinthians 10:5 (NIV)

What is a thought that sets itself up against the knowledge of God? It is a lie.

Jesus identifies the enemy of your soul as "The Father of lies" (John 8:44). Satan is fluent in fallacy and a master of misrepresentation. Deception is his first language. The disdain he possesses for God's creation is unrivaled.

He hates God and plans to destroy you (1 Peter 5:8). Working overtime to influence the way you think, the devil is playing for keeps. He plans to keep you afraid, doubting, and discouraged.

Repeated thoughts shape your beliefs and become the rooms in the house that is your heart. The gospel makes you powerful here and equips you to do the work necessary.

Tear down the lies, build up the truth. Frame up your mind in the best possible way and position yourself to overcome every obstacle in The Three Mile Valley. This is how you renovate and renew your mind.

Learning to think differently, like carving a new path through a field, takes time. The work is worth it because of the reward we get.

> *Do not conform to the pattern of this world, but be transformed by the renewing of your mind. Then you will be able to test and approve what God's will is—his good, pleasing and perfect will.* — Romans 12:2 (NIV)

When your mind is renewed, so is your vision. God empowers you to think the best thoughts. He knows what happens when you do. Let God help you think better through your valley. This cooperative effort is best achieved when you make time to read God's Word.

If you want to know what God is thinking, read the Bible. This simple discipline will renew your mind and further the good work that God is accomplishing in your life.

Marlena and I both regularly look to Scripture as we navigate The Three Mile Valley. We believe God knows what He is talking about. When we pay attention to what He says, we discover perspective that can sustain us through absolutely anything.

Identify your Path of Logic on the trail you take through The Three Mile Valley. Is it built on truth (God's Word)?

If it isn't, it is time to grab your sledgehammer and do some renovation between your ears. One key truth you can start with is this:

What you see is not what you get.
What you see is what you must get through.

Your now is not your forever. Moments like this have an expiration date…because God said so.

Watch "Now Is Not Forever"
at HopeBetweenTheLines.com

CONVERSATION STARTERS

Chapter Five Questions

Question: How would describe your Path of Logic?

What are some healthy thought habits you have?

____

____

____

____

____

____

____

____

Question: What thought patterns make you want to give up or leave you overwhelmed with doubts? How can you replace these with better—biblical—thinking?

____

____

____

____

____

____

____

Action: The Bible lets us know what God is thinking. If you are not already in God's Word daily, commit that for the next month you will read a portion of Scripture each day. If you aren't sure where to start, the Psalms and the Gospels (Matthew, Mark, Luke, and John) are great sources of comfort through a season of suffering.

"When life is good
we tend to have no questions,
but when life is bad
we have no answers."

Mike Mason

CHAPTER SIX

The First Mile: "Why?" is a Good Question

"The doctor said it's a tumor."

I froze as I held the phone to my ear. The sound of my wife's voice lacked its normal cheer and upbeat tone. Understandably, she spoke with somber clarity as she relayed this unsettling news to me.

Those six words hit me with the weight of sixty tons. Shocked by what this meant, I struggled to keep my composure as I stood in a public waiting area.

Months earlier, we noticed a small pea-sized bump above our youngest daughter's right eye. Once it became clear that it was not going away, we got Camdyn in to be seen immediately.

Whatever it was, her doctor said it needed to be removed. Before that could happen, they needed to know what was happening below the surface. That ultrasound showed a concerning sign; it was more than a bump. They ordered an MRI.

We wrangled for weeks and months with our insurance company to get the diagnostic test approved. Once approved, the scans gave the doctors a clear picture of everything happening under the surface.

Then, we waited for the results. One prayer I don't recommend anyone pray is, "God, please make me a patient person." You will be amazed at how fast heaven comes through for you.

Your answer will look a lot like an opportunity to wait, followed by more of the same.

When we finally got our answer, we heard the words no parent wants to hear. The bump above our daughter's eye was a tumor.

Camdyn was seven and had no idea what this might mean. Marlena and I knew full well what it *could* mean. We were intent to keep her uninformed of the negative possibilities until the surgery.

Only the biopsy of this pea-sized mass would tell us the truth about the unnerving potential of the pebble growing under her skin. More than life itself, we needed to know *Was it cancerous?*

The weeks between that moment and the surgery took forever to pass. *Would the surgery go well? How will she take the news? WHAT WILL BE THE REPORT?* The waiting was the worst.

Until I knew what we were up against, my mind worked overtime to paint the worst-case scenario over and over. We knew there would be clarity once the tumor was removed and studied. This thought was a relief.

That is … until I considered what a bad report would mean.

Night after night I went to sleep wondering how it would all end. We'd already had a funeral for one daughter, and I didn't know if I could handle one more. This was all too much.

One thought helped me get through this stressful stretch. *Now is not forever.*

We knew the surgery would give us an answer. *What if the answer isn't good?* We decided that knowing the truth is better than floating in a sea of uncertainty. If it was bad news, we would have to trust that God is everything the Bible says He is.

A sense of peace filled my heart, even as my anxiety reached a fever pitch.

Will God give us more than we can handle? Yes. However, *He will never give us more than* ***He*** *can handle.*

God's got this, no matter what happens next.

The weeks after the removal surgery felt like someone placed *forever* on pause. Kind of like when you call your cell phone provider and are placed on hold. The gentle, yet upbeat jazz fusion melodies slowly bump in your ear. When the music breaks, you think *This is it! I get to talk to real person!*

Disappointment sets in as you hear the friendly computerized voice say, "Thank you for holding. We really appreciate your business…"

Finally, we got the call we'd been waiting for. Marlena's phone rang, and I knew by the way she answered that it was the hospital.

Yes, this is Marlena. The tone of her voice left no doubt; this was the moment we had been waiting for.

Have you ever had this happen before? A moment where you're right next to someone getting the critical information you desperately need to know over the phone? All you hear is one side of the conversation, and you're at the mercy of your imagination to fill in what the other person is saying.

Uh-huh. Yes. Okay. Thank you.

All these words are not enough to provide context. Although the call lasted a few minutes, it felt like three hours. I heard her voice shift: *It's not cancerous?*

I felt the relief of a hundred and twenty thousand pounds lifting off my shoulders. My baby girl was going to be all right.

A question that vexes me to this day is, "Why, God, did you let that happen?"

You've asked that question too. We all ask that question. Even though the answer to this question will not change our circumstances, we still ask it. *Why, God? Why?*

It's a good question to ask, but is it the best question?

The Well of "Why?"

The first mile of The Three Mile Valley holds a place that represents our honest response to hard times. Welcome to The Well of "Why?"

Metaphorically speaking, it is an old-style, stone-walled well with a bucket resting on the rim. Everyone stops here because we have all been in situations that make us ask "Why?"

You see a sign affixed to the top of the well. It reads: *The Well of "Why?"* Just below is fine print that reads: *If you have a question, lower the bucket.*

What could it hurt? So, you lower the bucket deep into the dark cavern below. A loud splash greets your ears at it hits the bottom. The rickety container disappears under the water as it fills up.

As the bucket ascends the circular shaft of the well, it grows oddly lighter. By the time the bucket gets to the top, it is empty. A closer look reveals a large hole in the bottom.

Will working harder and faster to the draw the bucket back to the top bring relief? Maybe.

The irony is the thirst-quenching satisfaction you expected is replaced with greater thirst, and deeper fatigue.

This is the paradox that is The Well of "Why?" Sometimes asking "Why?" creates more questions than it does answers.

We ask *"Why?"* when pain prevents progress. As our circumstance sounds more like nails on a chalkboard than a soothing song, we ask it again.

Why did they leave?

Why did this have to happen to me?

Why can't I have what I want?

What you *want* when you ask "*Why?*" is an answer. What you *need* is strength for the next step.

God spoke to this suffering question long before we could ask it.

> *"My thoughts are nothing like your thoughts," says the LORD. "And my ways are far beyond anything you could imagine. For just as the heavens are higher than the earth, so my ways are higher than your ways and my thoughts higher than your thoughts."* —Isaiah 55:8–9 (NLT)

God sees things differently than we do. His perspective is unconstrained by space and time. He has no limits on how far back He can see. And looking forward, God can comprehend every future possibility.

That's impressive when you give it some thought. Our Creator exists on a whole other level, far beyond our finite mind's ability to understand. Yet, He comes close to us to help us through life.

Let's imagine God explained why He allowed you to suffer as you walk through The Three Mile Valley. As a part of the answer, He live-streams a full multimedia presentation down to your smartphone. It is complete with a sharp explainer video with eye-popping graphics and animations.

It is all broken down in plain language, and you have all the time you need to think it through.

As a bonus, God takes all your follow-up questions. At the end of this exchange, you would understand God's reasoning for allowing what you wish He didn't.

Here is where reality meets us. Would you be content? Did you really want God to give a full account for His divine activity, or lack thereof, from your view?

This is a hypothetical exercise, but I think it reveals something important—how we respond when the answer we receive is not what we want to hear.

More times than I can count, I have wondered why God allowed my daughter to die. If God explained His logic to me, I am confident I would still disagree with Him.

The biggest reason why is that I am not Him. I don't have His wisdom, compassion, or timeless perspective. You would not find me nodding my head in agreement, saying "That makes sense, God. Do You want my other children too?"

More than an answer, I want my pain to stop. My finite mind assumes that the limitless God could easily author another outcome for us.

Additionally, if I believe that God is the one who *causes* all my pain, then I am left to reconcile what that means.

Does Everything Happen for a Reason?

The Lord's Prayer begins with the well-known phrase, "Our Father in heaven, hallowed be your name" (Matthew 6:9, NIV). Jesus is teaching us how to pray here.

He intentionally begins by identifying God as a heavenly father. Yes, God is the creator, our judge, deliverer, redeemer, and more. The fact that Jesus teaches us to see God as our heavenly father is key.

He will discipline us (Hebrews 12:7) and develop us (John 15:1–2) because He is a good father.

Does this mean every single thing happens to us because God makes it happen?

In response to our loss, several people told us, "Everything happens for a reason." These words have created deep pain in me, and many others.

If it is true, that means that God *causes everything* to happen. Rapists rape, murderers murder, and liars lie – because God has planned it that way?

That thought cripples faith. How do you pray to a god who causes all your pain? This lie assails the goodness of God and stands in defiance of what the Scriptures reveal in totality about Him.

Evil is never His idea.

The deafening question that roars from the depths of my soul is "What about free will?" Starting back in the Garden of Eden, our Creator gave us the ability to choose our way forward.

The trust He's placed in us is so powerful that it includes the latitude to *not* love Him back. Why? He desires a real love with us. You can't have true love without true choice.

If you subtract this ability to pick and choose, you are left with nothing more than a robotic reality. We are far more complex than lines of code in a computer main-frame, wouldn't you agree?

This life is a gift from God Himself. What we do with it echoes past the edges of ourselves and ripples into the lives of everyone around us. This is the power of choice God placed in our hands from the moment we arrived.

Is a parent held accountable for everything their child does? Every parent feels the weight of their child's choices and works tirelessly to equip them to make the right ones. To be kind, courteous, and courageous in everything they do.

With that said, it is widely accepted that a parent is not responsible for their son or daughter's every decision.

This brings us to a second cliché we have all heard too many times: Everything happens for a reason. The truth about God's role in your pain is far more loving than that.

God does not make everything happen for a reason; He gives a purpose to everything that happens.

Your Creator is not toying with us by lobbing circumstances at us to see how we do. Everything is not a test, even though we are tested.

God cares so much for us that He lets people choose their way through life. Then, He sovereignly works out all situations for our good and His glory. Even the hard things.

God alone is powerful enough to take the exponential potential of your experience and make sense of it all. He does not *make* everything happen for a reason; He *gives* everything that happens a purpose.

When you embrace this truth, you pray differently. You know the Creator is not the source of all your pain. Instead, you see Him as the hope for all your healing.

Believing that God will give a purpose to everything that happens in your life changes your life because it changes your mind. You set yourself up to get your "*Why?*" along the way.

Knowing that now is not forever, you understand there is still time for God to work it all out for your good and His glory.

Scripture that supports this bold way of thinking is found in the book of Romans. It has given me great hope for my journey through The Three Mile Valley.

And we know that for those who love God all things work together for good, for those who are called according to his purpose.
— Romans 8:28 (ESV)

This powerful promise is for you. When you love God, your pain has a purpose. Your heavenly father goes to work on your behalf in every situation. Forging a future that is good for you because He loves you.

Should we stop asking *"Why?"* I don't think so. With that said, we should not stop living our life until we get an answer. We're here for so much more than this moment.

While The Three Mile Valley is an awful place to be, it is not where you will stay.

Watch "'Why?' is a Good Question"
at HopeBetweenTheLines.com

CONVERSATION STARTERS

Chapter Six Questions

Question: Have you ever been stuck at the Well of "Why?" Did it ultimately help or hinder your healing? Why is it so difficult to accept that we will never know *why* some things happen?

____

____

____

____

____

____

____

____

Question: "God does not make everything happen for a reason; He gives a purpose to everything that happens." How is this statement consistent with both God's sovereignty and man's free will? Why is it important to see God as the Redeemer instead of the Author of our pain?

____

____

____

____

____

____

____

____

____

Action: It's time to leave the Well of "Why?" behind! As you continue your journey, focus on the purpose with which God infuses your pain. Look for specific ways to use your pain productively—to help others in their suffering.

"Resilient people don't walk between the raindrops;
they have scars to show for their experience.
They struggle—but keep functioning anyway."

Hara Estroff Marano

CHAPTER SEVEN

The First Mile: "How?" Is the Best Question

Wrestling with questions is a healthy part of the journey through The Three Mile Valley. But there is one question that, when answered, will help you find the road map to victory.

How can I wisely get through this valley?

This pivot away from every other question is where spirituality and practicality intersect. Our response to this question is very important, because faith flows from an active response to God's Word.

When you reach up to grab Jesus' hand, you embark on a unique journey, full of both the miraculous and the mundane. Simultaneously awe-inspiring and awful, it is paradoxical at its core.

Read the words of Jesus here as He outlines the terms of His offer:

> *Then Jesus said to his disciples, "Whoever wants to be my disciple must deny themselves and take up their cross and follow me. For whoever wants to save their life will lose it, but whoever loses their life for me will find it. What good will it be for someone to gain the whole world, yet forfeit their soul? Or what can anyone give in exchange for their soul? For the Son of Man is going to come in his Father's glory with his angels, and then he will reward each person according to what they have done."*
> — Matthew 16:24–27 (NIV)

You and I are called to deny ourselves and carry our cross in every season of life. Just because we are suffering does not mean we should put our cross down.

Suffering well is the call of the cross in every circumstance we will ever face.

The Three Mile Valley is, quite vividly, our opportunity to identify with the suffering of our Savior and to become more like Him.

As we carry our cross forward, the old sinful "self" inside each of us decreases and Christ increases. In other words, abundant death to self-centered living makes ample room for Jesus to resurrect abundant life in us and release it through us.

The inspired writer of Philippians captures the essence of our pilgrimage this way:

> *I want to know Christ—yes, to know the power of his resurrection and participation in his sufferings, becoming like him in his death, and so, somehow, attaining to the resurrection from the dead.* — Philippians 3:10–11 (NIV)

Suffering is not a probability; it is a promise with a purpose. And that purpose, regardless of the details specific to each of our lives, is ultimately to bring us closer to Jesus.

Let this truth sink in! Our pain makes us the pupil in the classroom of life.

And here is the lesson we all must learn: In The Three Mile Valley, *we gain* through loss, setback, and disappointment. Pain's power is restrained by the hand of God as He guides us closer to Himself.

One of the fastest ways to get to know someone else is to suffer with them. This simple yet challenging exercise provides insight and perspective to another person that you might not gain any other way.

In the same way, hardship is a fast track to a closer walk with Jesus. You discover Him in despair, and you meet Him in the mess as He holds you through your moments of hell on earth.

God may not have authored your pain, but He will author good things *through* your pain.

Suffering is not a probability;
it is a promise with a purpose.

Thinking better thoughts is key to conquering The Three Mile Valley. When your thoughts are saturated with the truth, you have what you need to proceed in victory.

This in no way implies that suffering will be *easier* when you think better thoughts. By definition, suffering is hard. When you suffer well you will still shed tears, cry out in frustration, and come face to face with the real and raw you.

Cultivating a healthier Path of Logic through The Three Mile Valley allows you to hold fast to the promises found in God's Word.

This intentional choice to think better focuses your mind on the One who has already conquered the world. He is greater than your deepest valley, and now walks alongside you.

Your perspective will either precede or prevent perseverance in your life.

When your mind is aligned with the truth, you can overcome anything and everything that stands in your way. You owe it to yourself to think better thoughts through The Three Mile Valley. Embracing the fact that suffering is a part of the faith that saves you empowers you to ask the best question as you face suffering: How?

Focusing on *how* you will suffer is practical and productive. Like guardrails on a road, this question will drive you forward and keep you from veering off into other places that won't help you get to where you ultimately need to be.

I have sometimes found that my response in The Three Mile Valley is the only thing I can control.

You need to shift your focus from asking why God would allow pain to asking the best question instead: *How can I live well through this moment?*

When you ask this question, you position yourself to gain more than you could ever lose. Your thoughts will flow in the most productive direction possible: forward.

CONVERSATION STARTERS

Chapter Seven Questions

Question: How do you feel about the concept of suffering well? Do you think it is possible to live wisely even in extremely difficult circumstances? Why or why not?

____

____

____

____

____

____

____

____

Question: "Suffering is not a probability; it is a promise with a purpose." How does this statement affect your attitude toward suffering?

Action: Develop a personal mission statement of how you plan to walk through The Three Mile Valley. Make your statement succinct and easy to remember, as well as something that can bring you back to a faith-filled perspective on difficult days.

"What we say to ourselves is vitally important...
The good news is that we can change
the way we talk to ourselves
in order to harness the power
of self-compassion."

Nir Eyal

CHAPTER EIGHT

The First Mile: Remember Who You Are

When I was in elementary school, I loved to ride my bike. Here, there, and everywhere. My BMX style bike was pretty rad. The gray plastic wheel inserts covered up the spokes, and the tires had black racing style accents. The baseball card taped next to the back tire made it sound like I was ripping around on a dirt bike.

One day I was pedaling as fast I could to meet my friends to play. I tore across the parking lot of my apartment complex and was standing for maximum coolness.

As I pumped the pedals up and down, turning the handle- bars left and right, something unexpected happened.

My chain flew off the front sprocket, and the back tire grabbed. The bike stayed still, I did not.

Before I knew it, I was flying over the front wheel, Superman style. Skidding across the pavement on my chest brought me to a dead stop.

Pain was everywhere. My chest was on fire and the palms of my hands felt like they had exploded. However, neither of those places screamed the loudest.

The greatest ache came from the back of my right leg, near the calf muscle. Blood dripped down into my socks as I took stock of the situation.

My eyes shot wide open as I discovered multiple holes in my skin. Freshly punctured in a straight line and spaced out like the teeth of my bike's front sprocket. Somehow, my leg connected perfectly with the saw-like circle as I sailed over the handlebars.

In time, the back of my leg healed, and a line of small circle scars appeared. These marks remind me of what happened, but they do not define me.

I wrecked my bike, but I did not destroy my worth by having an accident. I have scars. They do not have me.

You are more than the sum of your scars.
You are held by the One who holds the stars.

Walking through The Three Mile Valley is difficult. You will accumulate your share of scars as you journey forward. Each one is a permanent reminder of a bad experience, but the pain will pass.

Remember, you are not your scars. You belong to the One with nail scarred hands.

Your tragedy is not your identity.

The world tells us that the defining power of pain in our lives cements who we are. Because of Jesus, however, we can differentiate who we are from what we go through. We must not confuse our identity with our experiences.

After Peyton passed, I discovered that my valley wanted to take more than my daughter from me. It reached for the very essence of who I was and still am.

Over time I lost sight of the truth about my identity. I forgot who God said I was.

This created an ugly pride inside of me. I allowed my identity to shift away from the foundation of God's Word and onto the shifting sands of circumstance.

Pride grew inside me because I thought that I was a survivor. This affected everything. I looked at myself differently. I looked at others differently.

I was wrong. I am not a survivor. A survivor's identity is rooted in the past. It is connected to something they can never change. This identity permeates everything. Like a badge proudly worn—it is on full display for everyone to see.

Jesus didn't come to make you a survivor. He came to make you a conqueror. The difference is dynamic.

Jesus doesn't ask us to live through hard times; He calls us to overcome them with Him.

> *No, in all these things we are more than conquerors through him who loved us.*
> — Romans 8:37 (NIV)

Remember who you are as you walk through The Three Mile Valley. Hear the declaration of scripture that boldly declares who you really are—more than a conqueror.

A survivor you are not! You are more than a conqueror in Christ. His victory has changed your identity in every circumstance. You are now an unstoppable overcomer in Christ.

Living in victory is more than what you do; it is the overflow of who you are through Him who loves you.

Your identity is not circumstantial;
it is providential.

You may feel like your situation is a complete loss. Because you are a conqueror, however, you need to fight until the end.

If there is time, you have a choice to make. Believe the truth about yourself and know that you will overcome your darkest day, even when it feels like it is fading into a darker night.

On the cross, Jesus was crowned the Victor. Through the cross, that crown benefits us. Please don't miss this!

Center who you are on Christ. When you do, you will know beyond a shadow of a doubt that your identity is not up for debate.

I love the way the Holy Spirit gets into the valley with us and reminds us of who we are. Read the following verses from Romans and see for yourself.

> *The Spirit himself bears witness with our spirit that we are children of God, and if children, then heirs—heirs of God and fellow heirs with Christ, provided we suffer with him in order that we may also be glorified with him.*
> — Romans 8:16–17 (ESV)

We are identified as the children of God in our suffering. The inheritance we now qualify for is eternal. We are merely passing through as we make our way to the full and abundant life Jesus purchased for us.

What if your valley is a result of your own doing, like the scar of a little boy who wrecked his bike?

I know what you might be thinking. You believe your actions are too much for God to redeem. That your mess is too messy for God to still love you.

Here's good news for you. Setbacks, mistakes, and heartaches authored by your own hand lose their suffocating power when you know who you are. God's grace is sufficient for you, even when you make mistakes.

Your identity in Christ is stronger than any string of bad decisions.

You are not the sum of your mistakes. You are not your scars. You are not destined to fail. You have been called to win, so press on until the end.

The Three Mile Valley will undeniably shape you, but it does not have to define you. Think helpful not hurtful thoughts and remember that who you are has nothing to do with where you are or what you are going through.

Now is not forever. You are more than a conqueror in Christ.

Watch "Remember Who You Are"
at HopeBetweenTheLines.com

CONVERSATION STARTERS

Chapter Eight Questions

Question: What scar(s) from the past have you allowed to define you? How does that definition of your identity differ from Christ's identity for you?

____

____

____

____

____

____

____

____

Question: How does taking on the identity of "more than a conqueror" change your perspective on your circumstances?

____

____

____

____

____

____

____

____

Action: Make a list of the identity traits that you have received in Christ, as found in Scripture (e.g., "I am accepted in the Beloved," "I am a new creation," "I am more than a conqueror"). Write or print out the list and put it in a place where you will see it often.

"It's far better to create your own future, repeatedly,
than to wait for external forces
to dictate your choices."

Jim Collins

CHAPTER NINE

The Second Mile: Cherish Your Choice

A while back, I was returning from El Salvador at the end of a short-term mission trip. An El Salvadoran woman was seated across the aisle from me. I speak some Spanish, and confess I had eavesdropped, picking up the light conversation she had with her husband and daughter earlier in the flight.

As the flight began its final approach, the woman started to fidget with the armrests. Her speech climbed in intensity and frequency. It didn't take a doctor to see that she was full blown panicking.

Suddenly, the cabin lights went dark. As the altitude of the jet went down, her anxiety ramped up.

Dimming the cabin lights is standard protocol for landing, but it was an unwelcome change for her.

I heard her whisper under her breath, "*Dios mio!*" ("Oh my God!"). She ferociously grabbed the armrests with a kung-fu death-grip.

Then, vapor clouds began to pour out of the ceiling ventilation system. This is completely normal and is caused by atmospheric changes. I thought it looked cool in the dimly lit atmosphere. Not so for *Nancy Nerviosa*.

We hit a bump in our descent, and she screamed "*Ay!*" as she braced herself. She was terrified!

Further and further down we went, until the back wheels of the plane touched the runway—and then the front wheels. She couldn't take much more.

It's a good thing we were almost done. As the plane touched down and glided across the runway, she employed her invisible plane brake pedal on the floor in front of her. It's the same kind your mom used when you were learning to drive.

Man, did Mrs. Nerviosa stomp on that imaginary braking system! Any harder and she might have kicked someone in first class.

The plane drew down to a safe and slow taxiing speed, and she let out a "*Gracias a Dios!*" ("Thank You, God!").

I said *yes* and *amen* to that.

What if *Nancy Nerviosa* had been unable to keep herself together? Who would have helped her?

The flight attendants would have. They oversaw the flight because they were stewarding it. Fully committed to responding to whatever might happen, these women and men help us understand what it means to make the best out of every situation.

In the second mile of our journey, we discover that thinking better is only part of the equation. Learning to do better as things get worse is the main theme here.

While we can't change what has happened, we can influence what happens next.

Cherish Your Choice – Choose Better

If your life is like an airplane ride, you are the steward. We live better through pain and heartache when we understand that we are responsible for our response.

Sometimes a season of suffering is our fault; other times it isn't. Regardless, we can steward our season *well* and experience goodness amid the bad.

As we follow the Master Valley Walker, Jesus, we aim to live with wisdom. Look at these verses from Ephesians that shape how we should see our journey through The Three Mile Valley.

> *Be very careful, then, how you live—not as unwise but as wise, making the most of every opportunity, because the days are evil.*
> — Ephesians 5:15-16 (NIV)

Your valley is full of opportunities. While it may not feel like it, every step forward is another opportunity to make the most out of your valley.

You owe it to yourself to make wise choices when life is hard.

Your loved ones benefit when you do this too.

God is glorified when you endeavor to make every choice throughout your Three Mile Valley a wise one.

Your response is your responsibility.

No one else can steward your valley for you. There isn't another individual who will be held responsible for the way you go through your valley. You cannot always control your circumstances, but you can consistently choose how you live through it.

You can live knowing that you have a significant part to play in your story. By doing this, you commit to carrying what you alone can carry. Your response to hardship is your responsibility.

This truth is both liberating and sobering, wouldn't you agree?

It is liberating because you know that you do have a choice in the matter. Even though circumstances may instigate a sense of chaos, God has given you a powerful gift during the storm: your response. What you do is up to you.

It is also sobering because you sense the weight of ownership that your choices create. God's grace will be enough for you on your darkest day. Should your response be unwise, God will faithfully walk with you through the reality of the consequences.

However, God's grace is not a license to be unwise, nor will it magically prevent the natural and negative outcomes of our poor choices.

What we do in difficult times matters more than we know. To make it through The Three Mile Valley, we must cherish our choice.

Choose wisely because you are worth it, no matter what.

When you do, the strength that remains in you will be channeled into choices that help you.

You don't have to make things harder than they already are. By God's grace, you can steward your difficult seasons in a way that leads to life after loss.

Watch "Cherish Your Choice"
at HopeBetweenTheLines.com

CONVERSATION STARTERS

Chapter Nine Questions

Question: What does it mean to steward your suffering? How can you gauge whether you are utilizing this stewardship wisely?

____

____

____

____

____

____

____

____

Question: What are some of the messes that often accompany a season of suffering? What are healthy outlets for strong emotions brought on by suffering?

____

____

____

____

____

____

____

____

Action: Try a new activity or opportunity that will give you a healthy release of anger/grief and empower you to make the better decision in your valley.

"We're very good at knowing what it is
we want right now; far less good at
predicting whether the object of our desire
will produce the satisfaction we take for granted."

Abigail Shrier

CHAPTER TEN

The Second Mile:
Defang Discontent Before It Bites

On December 11, 2008, Bernie Madoff shocked the world. No one had ever seen a swindle of this magnitude. His arrest dominated headlines and drove breaking news segments. Images of Bernie perp-walking in handcuffs made the news cycle in 24-hour rotations for weeks following.

Sadly, the damage he inflicted on the hard-working Americans who trusted him with their financial futures was done. To this day, individuals from nearly every level of society are still waiting for the money he promised to them.

A pension fund for firefighters and police officers lost up to $40 million.[3] Elie Weisel's foundation lost $15 million.[4] One investor, whose losses rocketed to $1.4 billion, ended up taking his life in the aftermath.[5]

The size of Madoff's Ponzi scheme is reported to have ballooned to $65 billion. Cracks in his deceptive empire were visible for years but managed to stay just below the surface of public scrutiny.

When the financial collapse of 2008 crushed the financial well-being of millions, waves rippled to the very foundation of his mountain of lies.

As his investors rushed to withdraw their money, he struggled to bring in enough fresh money to cover the furious outflows.

By the end of the year, the long-running con ran out of runway and crashed. The wreckage was incalculable and simply overwhelming.

We ask, "What could drive a person to be so selfish, or evil?" There are confirmed reports that Bernie used his Jewish faith to lure fresh victims into the scheme. Personality scientists will be combing through the carnage of his crimes for evidence of disorders for decades. I will leave that work to the professionals.

The ugly truth about what drove Bernie Madoff to take advantage of innocent people also lurks in the shadows of our souls. By the time his nefarious structures were in place, he was fully and undeniably justified in his own mind.

He knew what he was doing was wrong but did not seem to care. Going on record, Bernie "acknowledged his cognizance of the holes left in the regulatory environment, as well as the funding and personnel inadequacies, which he exploited in the maintenance of his Ponzi." [6]

In plain English, he knew what he was doing was wrong. He did it anyway because could get away with it. Choosing instead to blame the victim *and the enforcer* for his crimes, he was remorseless. That is, until he was caught.

At 71 years old, and facing 150 years of prison behind bars, Bernie would confess, "I cannot offer an excuse for my behavior." [7] Admitting this, after the damage has been done, cannot untangle the wreckage of his scheme as it lay in a heap of burning hopes, dreams, and security.

What drove Bernie Madoff to this level of deception? You could guess greed is at the heart of this twisted tale, and you'd be right.

I would add that he was self-justified in the scariest sense of the word. He blindly believed that his happiness was more important than anything else. People became pawns and were used to get him more of what he wanted.

Every one of his victims lost a game they never knew they were playing. When the law finally put Bernie in checkmate, the gig was up, and his house of cards came tumbling down.

A while back, I was in a conversation with a good friend who shared a profound insight with me. We were discussing the destructive decisions that another person was making.

Like Madoff, this person's web of lies collapsed in on them. Their family and friends found themselves in a world of hurt they didn't know was possible. We were heartbroken over the devastation that resulted from his choices.

I asked *Why would he ever think that was okay to do?* My friend pondered this question for a moment and then replied, "*Discontentment leads to entitlement.*" This is the genesis of every heartbreaking end. Let that revelation sink in for a moment.

Is discontentment always bad? Not necessarily. Nearly a decade ago, I stepped on my bathroom scale and was startled by the number staring back at me. It was the most I had ever weighed. Gulping at this sight, I became discontent because that number was unhealthy for me. Since that day, I leaned into that discontentment and made changes.

Discontentment becomes destructive when it drives you away from wisdom. This wreckage rests in smoldering piles all along the way when you let these paths of logic turn into habits and actions.

This powerful thought pattern, the one that magnifies all that is wrong and blinds you to all that is right, doesn't stay put in the soul. It moves you into entitlement thinking that sets the stage for more loss in your life.

When you're convinced you're supposed to have what no one promised you, you think differently—and destructively.

One of the most misunderstood Bible verses is Jeremiah 29:11. Often quoted by Christians in America, it devastatingly drives discontentment in the heart of believers all over the nation.

It says, "For I know the plans I have for you," declares the LORD, "plans to prosper you and not to harm you, plans to give you hope and a future" (NIV).

This statement from God was a shocking revelation of His goodness to those who originally heard it thousands of years ago. Why? God's people were languishing in captivity under the oppressive hand of the Babylonian empire. They only knew suffering. Hopelessness hung in the air around them like a thick stench all day, every day.

The Lord spoke this word to remind them that goodness flows from the essence of who He is, and that He had not forgotten them. He spoke those words right after He said, "When seventy years are completed for Babylon, I will come to you and fulfill my good promise to bring you back to this place."

When was the last time you waited seventy years for anything? I know that I get impatient sitting for seven seconds in the drive through as I pause in front of the speaker to give my order.

Seven decades. That's how long God was going to make His children wait before He stepped in to save them. Yet, this was good news to His people as they persevered in exile.

It is important we acknowledge that God never promised us the life we want deep down in our hearts. Instead, He promises to resurrect our spiritually dead hearts to full life through the power of the gospel (Ephesians 2:1).

Everything else in life is a beautiful bonus. Let me say this a bit more explicitly, so there is no room for confusion: God doesn't owe anyone anything.

Rather than that thought distancing us from Him, it should drive us deeper into our relationship with Him. All we are and have, all we can count on, is purely from His extravagant love for us.

I was talking with a friend the other day when he asked, "Dan, don't you ever get tired of all the challenges you and your family face?" He went on to explain that it seems like the Herod family has endured an inordinate amount of pain and difficulty. More than most, he would say.

I recounted the "big ones" that have shaken me to the core:

-Walking alongside Marlena as she suffers debilitating migraines for over twenty years.

-Enduring temporary facial paralysis from a bout of Bell's Palsy.

-Two miscarriages, which happened back-to-back.

-Losing my middle daughter to SIDS at thirteen months.

-Seeing my youngest daughter develop a tumor above her eye that had to be surgically removed.

-Rushing to the hospital after that same daughter had a twenty-five-minute seizure and spending the night wondering if she will ever be the same. (She came through and is all right.)

I understood what he was getting at. That is a lot by most measurements. While I do wish God would have prevented all of these—all of them—from happening, in the core of who I am I believe this following truth: God doesn't owe me anything.

In salvation, He's already given me the very thing I need more than anything else.

Please hear me when I say this: I don't secretly hope God backs a dump truck of suffering at the edge of my world and lets even more rain down on me.

I am actively fighting the devastating twisted path of "logic" called "entitlement" with every ounce of my being. I know where that trail leads, and it is nowhere good.

False thoughts, when allowed to linger, will lead us down a path we don't want to tread. Here are some examples of false thinking in The Three Mile Valley:

- I have lost everything.
- He/she owes me.
- I will never be happy again.
- I no longer have purpose.
- I can't make it without (whatever or whoever you lost).
- I am nothing without (whatever or whoever you lost).
- I can't forgive myself.
- I can't forgive them.

It's not wrong to think these thoughts. I have repeatedly wrestled each of them. You will go through the full spectrum of grief as you cope with suffering. That is okay, and you should not feel guilty for that.

It is also okay for you to break free from the dangerous cycle that these thoughts can create. You owe it to yourself to think true thoughts in The Three Mile Valley. That is the essence of your journey through the first mile.

When you think better, you can choose better. This is the essence of the second mile.

When you stop the slide that entitlement thinking creates, you halt the descent into unbridled justification. This is where Bernie Madoff arrived before he began his swindle. It is here that he cultivated the reasoning for his ruse.

The sobering truth is that no one is immune from the allure of a self-justified mindset. Not me, and not you.

Justification takes place when biblical logic leaves the conversations you have with yourself. When you descend into this thought dungeon, you will do things you said you would never do. What you once considered wrong is now right.

Here is where so many people walking through The Three Mile Valley create additional pain and loss for themselves. Regretfully, it doesn't stay inside of them. Just like an explosion sends shockwaves reverberating out, the consequences of justified choices smash into the lives of innocent bystanders.

Quite often, those we hurt the most in this moment are the ones we love the most: our friends and family.

This crater ringed by ruins will never be the same because people don't heal like buildings do. You can't just replace the walls, slap a new coat of paint and roof on a relationship.

While reconciliation and redemption are possible in every situation, they are not promised. You and I need to get to the root of this in our own hearts and deal with it before it grows legs and starts running amuck.

It all starts with a thought.

Kill discontentment before it kills everything and everyone you love. To forge a new path of logic that is healthy spiritually, emotionally, and relationally, you can look to the Bible.

The book of Philippians speaks to the power of contentment in your circumstances:

> *...for I have learned to be content whatever the circumstances. I know what it is to be in need, and I know what it is to have plenty. I have learned the secret of being content in any and every situation, whether well fed or hungry, whether living in plenty or in want. I can do all this through him who gives me strength.*
> —Philippians 4:11b–13 (NIV)

You can put yourself on a path toward contentment as you walk through The Three Mile Valley. Here are the three steps:

1.) Contemplate the truth that Christ is enough. When you meditate on this reality, you align your mind with the truth. This new path of logic sets the direction for the rest of your life and will serve you long after you've left this valley. In any and every circumstance, you need to hold fast to the truth that Christ is enough.
2.) Center your hope on Jesus and His promises. This is gospel-driven empowerment. This is the "I can do all things through Christ" reality that contentment secures for us. Because Christ is all we need, we are driven to do more with what we have in our lives instead of waiting on the world to change before we act.
3.) Choose to be a conduit of life for everyone around you. The beautiful outcome of gospel-centered empowerment is abundant life in us, as it flows through us. Seasons of suffering can knock you down momentarily as you seek to find your bearings in the storms of life. But because Jesus is

> present, you don't have to stay down. You can rise and even thrive through your most painful experiences.

The benefits of contentment in your life cannot be overstated.

Because of Jesus, you are not at the mercy of your circumstances. You walk with the One who is bigger than everything you face.

Choose to embrace contentment in your valley, and watch God move in you and through you.

CONVERSATION STARTERS

Chapter Ten Questions

Question: How have you found yourself discontented in your season of suffering? What were some of the ways you responded? Would you do anything different?

____

____

____

____

____

____

____

____

Question: What are ways you can cultivate contentment in your current season of suffering?

____

____

____

____

____

____

____

____

____

Action: As you reflect on your current season, identify a concrete action you can take to further your journey through The Three Mile Valley.

"When gospel-fluent Christians suffer,
they understand that since it's all grace,
there's nothing God can't ask of them.
He owes us nothing, but gives us everything."

Pastor David Hertweck

CHAPTER ELEVEN

The Second Mile: Grace in the Fire

Twenty years. That is how long I've watched my wife suffer migraine headaches. They started during the first year of our marriage and have increased in frequency and duration. They've kept her in bed 20-25 days every month.

The saving grace for her is a new treatment we found a couple of years ago. It grants her eight weeks of relief. The kicker is that she can only get it every twelve weeks. This means she is sidelined for a month as she waits for the next round.

I have repeatedly and consistently prayed for her healing. Our friends and family all over the nation lift her up in prayer and regularly ask God for a complete healing.

To date, God has not answered the way we want Him to. He has answered though. Instead of coming through with a miraculous healing, He infuses us with a grace that gives us hope.

Sometimes God will give us what we need before He provides what we want.

The apostle Paul illustrates the ways in which God will sometimes answer our cries for relief with something else.

> *Three times I pleaded with the Lord to take it away from me. But he said to me, "My grace is sufficient for you, for my power is made perfect in weakness." Therefore I will boast all the more gladly about my weaknesses, so that Christ's power may rest on me. That is why, for Christ's sake, I delight in weaknesses, in insults, in hardships, in persecutions, in difficulties. For when I am weak, then I am strong.* —2 Corinthians 12:8–10 (NIV)

When Paul begged God to change his situation, God changed him instead.

Let that sit for a second.

The inconvenient truth about our Creator's ways is that they are different than ours (Isaiah 55:8).

God's grace goes to work in you as He wisely works out circumstances around you. This inner working perfects you from the inside out. If you're like me, you would like God to first make the world around us perfect before working on the inside.

You might be wondering how my wife survives these headaches. Does she ever get frustrated? You better believe it!

However, she manages the uncontrollable circumstance of her migraines by accepting that her response is her responsibility. When she is in pain, she quietly listens to uplifting music. If able, she reads passages of Scripture.

She knows that who you listen to when you suffer has the power to change your outlook, for better or worse. Understanding this, she chooses the better voice when she is down and out.

If light doesn't hurt her eyes too bad, she watches her favorite shows, reads avidly, and journals about her experiences.

She is regularly sidelined for weeks at a stretch, multiple times a year. Her chosen path of logic focuses on the relief that she will get at the next treatment.

Well-worn and walked-wide through countless trips down that path, she knows that the headache will eventually lift.

Her now is not her forever.

When it does lift, Marlena is up and out of the house, committed to living as much life as possible. She hangs out with friends, goes shopping, and attends church services.

Knowing that a headache-free day will soon come doesn't make her pain any less, but it does empower her to focus on what she can control while the headache is still present.

Watching Marlena navigate this season of suffering has been amazing. She decides to cherish her choice. While she can't prevent these headaches, she still possesses power to choose her way forward. A perfect picture of grace in the fire, my bride inspires me.

What if God doesn't answer our prayers for Marlena's complete healing? Lord knows, we have asked a thousand times. We do believe that it is only a matter of time before she will be completely free from the headaches that have taken so much from her.

But until that happens, we accept what is, cherish our choice, and trust in His presence to see us through.

In your own valley, it is important to remember that God is present. His presence promises provision in the pain.

When you focus on Him, and not what you expect from Him, you've set the stage for a true miracle.

CONVERSATION STARTERS

Chapter Eleven Questions

Question: As you go through your valley of suffering, what are you able to control?

____

____

____

____

____

____

____

Question: Are you committed to following Jesus even if He does not fix your situation or answer your prayers in the way you desire? How would you describe your commitment to Him?

____

____

____

____

____

____

____

____

Action: In your study group or with a Christian friend, share two prayers that God has answered recently—one that He answered in the way you desired and one that He answered in a way you did not prefer. What did you learn from each situation?

"God powerfully invades us when we
persevere patiently through this suffering.
Our great temptation is to quit or go backward,
but if we remain still, listening for his voice,
God will insert something of himself
into our character that will mark
the rest of our journey with him."

Peter Scazzero

CHAPTER TWELVE

The Second Mile: Mind Your Meds

I had a crush when I was in the eighth grade, long before I met Marlena. This middle school beauty had beautiful eyes and curly blond hair. Hailing from the south, she mesmerized my Midwest mind with her thick accent. Everything she said was pure magic.

I was smitten.

Determined to get her attention, and ultimately her affection, I decided to play a game of basketball with her. Let me be clear: I was not a good basketball player by any means. However, this Southern Belle was there. It was my time to transform into Luka Doncic and win her heart.

At one point during the game, I was driving into the lane for a layup. As I jumped, my feet tangled with another player's. I rotated midair and fell flat onto my back. A collective "oooohhhh" from the crowd filled the air and the game stopped.

Searing pain shot down both of my legs in that instant. The ache was immense, and it felt like someone hit me with a baseball bat right above my rump.

After a few moments of lying there, I was helped to my feet. I struggled to stand. Taking simple steps was a chore. Yet somehow, I managed to keep playing. Why? My crush was watching!

That moment changed my life, but not the way I hoped. I did not get the girl. Instead, I got a severe spinal injury.

Sitting in front of my doctor in disbelief, I learned that I had herniated a disc. The damage to my spine required surgery.

One day after my birthday, I went under the knife. As I closed my eyes, anesthesia pulled me under. I silently prayed *God please let this work* as I slipped away.

Waking up in the recovery room is an unforgettable experience. You're in a haze, stuck somewhere between awareness and looniness.

In the weeks leading up the procedure, I worried that something would go wrong, and that the surgeon would nick my spinal cord. If that happened, I was certain I would never be able walk again. I lost count of how many times I traveled on that path of logic. It was enough to give my doctor the scare of a lifetime as I came to.

Standing at the side of my bed, he began to speak. His words were punctuated by the steady beep of the heart monitor announcing the cadence of my pulse.

"Daniel, can you wiggle your toes for me?" He had done many surgeries and was an accomplished orthopedic specialist. I don't think he was prepared for what came out of my mouth.

My mind swirled like a tilt-a-whirl as I labored to find the words to answer his simple question. Because I had convinced myself before surgery that something was going to go wrong during the operation, I blurted out "I CAN'T MOVE MY LEGS!"

The doctor's voice snapped into a serious tone as he barked, "What do you mean?"

I mumbled incoherently.

Demanding a response, he commanded "Move your toes!"

Moments later, all ten of my little piggies wiggled wildly. His relief was evident, as was mine.

Medications can be quite powerful, which is why the most effective ones are prescribed by a medical professional. Some numb you, while others help heal you.

The drugs given to knock me out for the surgery did their job. So well in fact that my state of mind coming out of the operation was altered.

As you walk through The Three Mile Valley you need to mind your meds carefully. I am not just talking about the little pills you get from the pharmacy. This also includes the numerous ways you cope with tough times.

Everyone self-medicates in some way. In other words, we are all prone to turning to a myriad of things to numb the pain of our circumstances. This isn't always bad, but it can become unhealthy if what we turn to simply masks our symptoms and doesn't help us heal.

For most of us, the medication question isn't if, it's how and when.

Do you know which medications help your soul heal from the wounds of life? What about the things that disconnect us from reality, potentially injuring us further?

The Three Mile Valley is where spiritual medication can change everything for you.

Three powerful antidotes that also act as healing agents are available to you in abundance. They can help you manage your pain as you walk through your valley.

The Presence of God

The first medication God provides is His loving presence.

> *Not only so, but we also glory in our sufferings, because we know that suffering produces perseverance; perseverance, character; and character, hope. And hope does not put us to shame, because God's love has been poured out into our hearts through the Holy Spirit, who has been given to us.* — Romans 5:3–5 (NIV)

God pours a dose of help for you every single day. It is provided through the Holy Spirit. This heavenly love is unlike anything we can find here on earth. It is pure and powerful. It is free and full of life.

God's presence doesn't make our suffering disappear. But when we rest in God's presence, we can see that suffering is one of the ways God makes us stronger. In response to the pain, God gives us a hope that will not put us to shame.

To take this divine dose of medication, all you need to do is open up.

He is not a god who uses an eye dropper stingily to give us His love. The word *pours* from the verse above gives a clear picture of God lavishly showering you. He is love (1 John 4:8), and longs to saturate your heart with His loving presence to help you heal.

The Word of God

The second medication that God supplies is His Word. The Bible is not just *a* good book; it is *the* Good Book. It is more than print on paper and sentences on the screen of your digital device.

Look at Romans 15:4 (NIV). It says, "For everything that was written in the past was written to teach us, so that through the endurance taught in the Scriptures and the encouragement they provide we might have hope."

When you and I study the Bible, we learn endurance and receive encouragement. This prescription is predestined by God to give us hope.

You set yourself up for success when you read the Word of God.

> *Your word is a lamp for my feet, a light on my path.* — Psalm 119:105 (NIV)

His Word is a guiding light for everyday life. It illuminates our way through The Three Mile Valley. Often, just enough to help us see our next step.

The Bible is full of promises that apply to your path. Reading story after story of God's faithfulness to His children builds your faith. When you know what God can do, it isn't a matter of *if* He will, but *when* He will.

Let the Word of God illuminate each step you take through your difficult seasons. You will be able to walk with wisdom as you steward your season of suffering.

You will have help to see more of what is happening around you because the Bible is a lamp for your feet.

You never have to hold God to His promises. You only need to hold fast within them.

> *For the word of God is alive and active. Sharper than any double-edged sword, it penetrates even to dividing soul and spirit, joints and marrow; it judges the thoughts and attitudes of the heart.* — Hebrews 4:12 (NIV)

In addition to illuminating our circumstances, the Word of God is also penetrating. It cuts past our façades and gets to the heart of every matter. It introduces us to God's thoughts in ways that would otherwise be unattainable. It shows us our true reflection as we gaze into the mirror of its counsel.

> *Take the helmet of salvation and the sword of the Spirit, which is the word of God.*
> — Ephesians 6:17 (NIV)

There are going to be stretches of your valley that will require you to fight. The Word of God is the only offensive weapon we have for the battle.

You will need to have your sword ready to cut down the lies of your spiritual enemy, the devil. You will be equipped to suffer well when you walk with God's Word hidden in your heart.

> **Arm yourself** because the battle will be intense. **Encourage yourself** because you will win when you stand on God's Word.

Take this dose of medication by reading the Bible regularly. Read it in the valley. Read it outside of the valley. You will find God's grace preparing you for what lies ahead, so you can carry it with you in difficult times.

The People of God

The third medication that God gives us is His Church. Having a team is key to winning in every season. The Church is your God-given team.

Your "weekly huddle" may include twenty people or twenty-five thousand. Regardless of the size of the church, it is critical that you faithfully and regularly participate.

> *And let us consider how we may spur one another on toward love and good deeds, not giving up meeting together, as some are in the habit of doing, but encouraging one another—and all the more as you see the Day approaching.*
> — Hebrews 10:24–25 (NIV)

Too often we stop doing the things we need to do when life gets hard. Going to church is no exception. You cannot afford to stop attending church when you are walking through The Three Mile Valley. There is too much at stake.

Take a dose of this medication often. Your presence in the body of Christ is the prescription for your soul.

Every time you show up, you give God a chance to show off. He wants to reveal to you that you are not alone. He wants to show others in the body of Christ that suffering is a normal part of carrying one's cross.

This mutual edification brings authenticity to His Church.

Something powerful happens when we all know that we are not okay, but that it will all be okay. When you gather with others to worship, hear the teaching of the

Word, and connect with each other, you receive a healthy dose of medication for your journey.

Other Medications

There are other medications that are safe for you to rely on as you journey through The Three Mile Valley. Listen to the needs of your heart and body and take these things in moderation so they don't become unhealthy addictions or obsessions. Here are a few:

- Exercise
- Laughter
- Sleep
- Friendship
- Healthy food
- Work

Take each of these medications in addition to the Presence of God, the Word of God, and the People of God.

When you mind your meds, you set yourself up to make it all the way through The Three Mile Valley.

You owe it to yourself to medicate wisely in every season of life. When you do, you allow ample room for the life of Christ to fill every part of your soul. This presence inside of you is greater than anything you face outside of you.

Watch “Mind Your Meds”
at HopeBetweenTheLines.com

CONVERSATION STARTERS

Chapter Twelve Questions

Question: What are some helpful and unhelpful ways people seek to soothe their pain in suffering? Which of these "meds" have you used, and what were the results?

Question: How have the Presence of God, the Word of God, and the People of God brought you comfort in The Three Mile Valley?

____

____

____

____

____

____

____

____

Action: Ask a trusted friend if there are any areas of "self-medicating" in which you are off balance (e.g., working to exhaustion, over- or under-sleeping, over- or under-eating). Prayerfully consider any blind spots your friend points out and ask for accountability to use these "meds" in a healthy and balanced way.

"God wants to bring joy not pain,
peace not war,
healing not suffering."

Henri Nouwen

CHAPTER THIRTEEN

The Second Mile: Soul Rehab

After my back surgery, I went through a rehabilitation process. Learning how to live with pain as I progressed toward wholeness was not easy. My doctor told me to start doing the rehab exercises as soon as I was able.

Waiting until all my pain was gone was not an option. It was time for me to start building a life on the other side of my injury.

I was nowhere close to healed when the rehab process began. Some of the exercises were painful to do, but necessary if I wanted to recover completely.

This process was incredibly important because it impacted the rest of my life. I am living an active life today because of the choices I made in response to an injury I experienced in eighth grade.

How you and I steward the space and time between our loss and this moment directly impacts our healing. Our response in the valleys of life will either hasten or inhibit our healing.

God desires for you to be healed. When you cherish your choice, you hasten your healing. When you rehab your soul, you are giving God the time and space to heal you.

Time Heals Nothing

You have probably heard people say that "time heals all wounds." In my own journey through The Three Mile Valley, I have discovered this to be false.

Time possesses no magical power to heal any wound. The power that time does possess, however, creates space between the point of pain and your present reality.

If we expect time alone to heal our wounded souls, we will be waiting forever.

But there are concrete actions we can take to hasten our healing.

Your response to the adversity you face is important. God will do His part. He will author good things from the setbacks you endure.

Pain's power is quite persuasive. It tempts you to stay put until the agony subsides.

While this is wise in some scenarios, it is not the best choice in every situation.

The only thing stopped permanently as I wait for the pain to stop is me—life goes on.

To gain the advantage over your pain, all you need to do is put it into perspective. In Christ, you are permanent; your pain is not. Your season is temporary; you are not. Make decisions that shape a future you can thrive in, not ones that only apply to your temporary season.

Rehab Exercises

Four exercises assist us as we journey through The Three Mile Valley. They are meant to be done regularly and at our own pace, but steadily, consistently.

Exercise Faith

God doesn't need us to trust Him in order to be God. But we need to trust Him to *experience* Him as God.

> *Trust in the LORD with all your heart and lean not on your own understanding; in all your ways submit to him, and he will make your paths straight.* — Proverbs 3:5–6 (NIV)

As you walk through your valley, remember the promise found in this verse. God makes our path navigable when we trust Him, even when we don't understand.

Recently I flew to Vietnam with some friends. Our first flight was fourteen hours or so. It made our second flight, which was five hours, seem like a walk in the park.

On the fourteen-hour flight, I was struck by the realization that while I was sitting there, essentially waiting, we were still moving—and quite fast, I might add.

On that flight, I placed my trust in the pilot, and he rewarded my trust. The entire time I was seated, the pilot was making sure I was headed in the right direction.

What felt like waiting was getting me to where I needed to be.

The same is true for us as we "wait" in our seasons of suffering. When we trust the Lord, He works to get us where we need to be in ways that we could not do on our own.

While you are waiting, God is working.

> *But they who wait for the LORD shall renew their strength; they shall mount up with wings like eagles; they shall run and not be weary; they shall walk and not faint.*
> — Isaiah 40:31 (ESV)

When it feels like your faith in God has you sitting in a waiting room instead of walking forward on a path, it is okay. As you and I trust Him above everything else, we can be sure that everything will eventually work out.

Faith is not always an easy exercise, but it always brings us results we can live with.

Exercise Forward

The best way through The Three Mile Valley is forward. Why? Because now is not forever and this earth is not our eternal home. Consider what the apostle Paul says in the following verse.

> *I press on toward the goal to win the prize for which God has called me heavenward in Christ Jesus.* — Philippians 3:14 (NIV)

When you and I walk through The Three Mile Valley, we need to set our sights on heaven as we walk through hell on earth. We are passing through this space because it is not our permanent resting place.

Commit to moving forward, knowing you can never go back to the life you had outside The Three Mile Valley. When you do emerge from the valley, you will be different. Your world will be different.

There is a good *ever after* waiting for you because Jesus is working in you now. Every step you take forward brings you that much closer to the good that God is working through your seasons of suffering.

Every year following the loss of our daughter, we do this exercise as a family. It is an important part of rehab for our wounded souls.

On the anniversary of Peyton's passing, we go somewhere fun to make good memories on the date that will forever be full of painful ones.

So far, we have visited Disney World, Disneyland, the Wisconsin Dells, and Universal Studios Florida. We have even taken a Disney cruise. Is it a coincidence that we regularly visit the "happiest place on earth" on the worst date on our calendar? I think not.

We will never get over Peyton's passing, and we shouldn't. Instead, we will carry her memory forward with us as we heal along the way.

When you do this exercise, you declare that you choose to live through your pain. If you're grieving the loss of a loved one, I am not saying you should "get over it."

Grief is a journey that will lead you through multiple stages.

Denial, Anger, Bargaining, Depression, Acceptance and Assigning Purpose are all evolutionary points for your wounded soul in The Three Mile Valley.

It is common for those in grief to jump between stages and even return to stages of grief more than once. You don't have to pressure yourself to be at any specific point in this healing progression. You just need to focus on healing.

As you walk through your valley, exercise forward. It is one way you can cherish your choice and steward your season of suffering with wisdom.

God is not done writing your story. You will live even through loss, heartache, setback, and suffering. Resolve today to exercise well and move forward at your pace.

Exercise Forgiveness

Forgiveness is a key exercise you must perform if you want to suffer well through The Three Mile Valley. It is also a mandate for everyone who follows Jesus.

> *For if you forgive other people when they sin against you, your heavenly Father will also forgive you. But if you do not forgive others their sins, your Father will not forgive your sins.*
> — Matthew 6:14–15 (NIV)

Matthew 6:14 minces nothing as Jesus lays out the need for us to exercise forgiveness. You *must* forgive others if you want God to forgive you.

When you accept Jesus' invitation to follow Him, you drop your way to go His way. Should you refuse to forgive others for how they hurt you, you are walking the wrong way.

It is a path away from Jesus, and you risk losing more than you could ever imagine.

Unforgiveness is the opposite of all that Jesus is about. His way is forgiveness for all people and for everything they have done. He liberally offers forgiveness to everyone who asks.

The one who walks in His way is a primary benefactor of unreasonable grace on every level.

Bitterness is the unruly companion of the unforgiving heart. It takes up residence and seeps into every corner of our lives. When you activate the power of forgiveness, you sever the dark power of bitterness over your life.

Your path through The Three Mile Valley might be full of pain caused by the choices of another. In that case, this exercise in forgiveness could be difficult for you.

Invite Jesus into your pain and ask Him for help. Your confession of faith will usher grace directly into your soul.

When you admit your need, you receive the help of heaven. God wants you to walk in forgiveness, and He will provide everything you need to take each step.

Exercising forgiveness in The Three Mile Valley lightens your load exponentially. When you shed the excess weight of a bitter heart, you gain so much. You find freedom for every step that lies ahead.

Exercise Self-Forgetfulness

Serving others as you journey through The Three Mile Valley is counterintuitive. Quite often, God's ideas are.

> *Do nothing from selfish ambition or conceit, but in humility count others more significant than yourselves. Let each of you look not only to his own interests, but also to the interests of others.*
> — Philippians 2:3–4 (ESV)

We have been blessed to have great friends for our entire married life. For several years, we watched two of our good friends struggle to get pregnant. Our hearts broke for Gabe and Serah as they journeyed on the sustained path through The Three Mile Valley.

Shortly after Peyton's passing, we got the news that their twins were born. You read that right: twins.

Marlena and I decided to go and visit our friends and experience their doubly blessed reality for ourselves. We are so glad we did—their twin babies were adorable!

As is the custom, we brought gifts for our friends to celebrate their growing family.

Why did we do that? We had every reason to stay cocooned in our pain. No one would have judged us if we had chosen to stay away. However, something inside of us compelled us to make the trip.

Questions swirled through my mind as I thought through our visit beforehand. The most frightening question I wrestled with was, *Will the sight of a newborn remind us so strongly of our Peyton that we'll collapse in our grief rather than celebrate with them? How will I respond if we're overwhelmed?*

Those questions were fueled by fear, which did not want us reaching past our pain to bless someone else.

It was not easy to exercise self-forgetfulness, but when we did so, it was liberating. Although we went to give to our friends, we received so much more in return.

God's promise to you in the valley is clear. When you lift your eyes up and off your situation and serve those around you, your world is illuminated.

Self-forgetfulness is the call of the cross in every season of life.

The benefit of service during your suffering is life changing. Specifically, your life will change as you seek to help others change their lives. Exercising self-forgetfulness is key to suffering well through The Three Mile Valley.

This brings us to a third and final cliché we've all heard too many times: Times heals all wounds. If this were true, you would never meet a bitter senior citizen! Seriously though, time doesn't heal anything on its own.

The truth is this: What you *do* with time can heal everything.

This perspective is key for you and me if we want to live rich and meaningful lives in the face of deep loss and disappointment.

Rehab Well

To heal well in The Three Mile Valley, you need to rehab well. As you walk through the painful stretches, remember to cherish your choice, and steward your season well. Your healing is on the way.

Your soul can be made well when you exercise faith, forward movement, forgiveness, and self-forgetfulness.

Watch "Soul Rehab"
at HopeBetweenTheLines.com

CONVERSATION STARTERS

Chapter Thirteen Questions

Question: What is an example of a permanent choice someone might make in a temporary season? Why is this unwise? How can you be sure the Lord is guiding your decisions in the valley?

____

____

____

____

____

____

____

____

Question: Faith, Forward, Forgiveness, and Self-forgetfulness: Which rehab exercise is the easiest for you? Which is the hardest? Why?

____

____

____

____

____

____

____

____

Action: What is a tangible decision you can make to "exercise forward"? Or to "exercise self-forgetfulness" in ministering to someone else (perhaps even the person for whom you have been praying)? Begin planning or acting on this decision this week.

"The power of a moment makes it a source of
immeasurable opportunity and hope.
No matter what kind of life you've lived,
no matter how many wrong choices you've made,
the next moment is waiting to give birth to new life."

Erwin McManus

CHAPTER FOURTEEN

The Third Mile: There Is Always an After

You've made it to the third mile of our journey! The third mile welcomes us with hopeful signs of life and renewal.

If the first and second miles are about what you can do, the third mile is about what God is already doing on your behalf. Watching God make things better is the key to conquering this mile.

Losing our daughter suddenly at thirteen months has taught us much. One of the biggest lessons is that God is working it all out. His goodness to us guarantees that there is always an after.

> *And we know that God causes everything to work together for the good of those who love God and are called according to his purpose for them.* — Romans 8:28 (NLT)

"Everything will be okay in the end. If it's not okay, it's not the end."

This thought captures the essence of perspective. We are people of faith who trust in the One who is greater than everything we face.

When we suffer well, when we change our conversations about suffering, we live knowing that everything will eventually be okay. This brings us to our third and final principle.

There is Always an After—
Watch God Make It Better

God is the master of the after. He alone sits above time as He simultaneously walks with us right now. His perspective gives Him the ability to see well beyond this moment.

As God looks forward, He sees all that He can accomplish through your darkest times. He authors an after that is good and far beyond anything we could shape on our own.

The first *after* is eternity in heaven. The gospel gives us a hope beyond The Three Mile Valley. Jesus accomplished what we couldn't to give us what we can't live without. Before He ascended to heaven, Jesus gave us this promise:

> *"Do not let your hearts be troubled. You believe in God; believe also in me. My Father's house has many rooms; if that were not so, would I have told you that I am going there to prepare a place for you? And if I go and prepare a place for you, I will come back and take you to be with me that you also may be where I am. You know the way to the place where I am going."*
> — John 14:1–4 (NIV)

The hope of heaven is the best after we can have. There, we will discover all the preparations Jesus made for our arrival. This place is waiting for us and will be abundantly better than the life we have now.

It brings great comfort to know that Jesus prepared a place for Peyton long before she passed away. The after that Jesus created for her is beyond our wildest imagination. It is a good place, where her soul experiences God's fullness in ways we simply cannot comprehend.

Because of Jesus, Marlena and I will also experience this after.

Whenever we pass through the veil of eternity, we will be welcomed into an after that we did not earn or deserve. Any suffering we experienced in this life will cease in heaven.

> *God will wipe away every tear from their eyes; there shall be no more death, nor sorrow, nor crying. There shall be no more pain, for the former things have passed away.* — Revelation 21:4 (NKJV)

Heaven is the first after that we can look forward to as we journey through The Three Mile Valley. It is guaranteed to everyone who accepts Jesus' invitation to follow Him.

As you walk through The Three Mile Valley, you can know with certainty that the place Jesus has prepared for you is good.

It must be said that some who journey through The Three Mile Valley step into eternity because of the suffering they endure in the valley. They receive the fullness of heaven that Jesus promised them, and experience now what you and I can only imagine.

If heaven was the *only* after that God authored for us, that would be more than we deserved. This brings us to another after that God is faithfully working out on our behalf.

God is composing an alternate ending to your story. He has the last word, and it is often revealed after you walk through your darkest days. What God writes is good.

Though you may be grieving deeply over your losses, God is working to add something greater within you that no one can take away.

Even if it feels like the darkness has swallowed you whole, the light of eternity burning within you remains.

When God speaks the last word, nothing can stop His purpose from prevailing.

While life subtracts from you, God is adding to you. He is not stumped by our setbacks, stymied by our suffering, or derailed by death.

God adds through seasons of subtraction.

The beauty of Jesus' story is that it is an example of what God can do in your story.

After He was crucified, the world around Jesus' tomb continued to spin on. The soldiers standing guard outside the grave had no clue they were about to witness a resurrection. You see, the world thought the funeral was final, that the grave had the last word.

Then, after three days had passed, God authored an alternate ending the world did not expect. The ground began to shake, the stone was rolled away, and our Savior stepped out of the tomb.

Death was defanged the moment Jesus came roaring back to life.

The Master Valley Walker completed His conquest of The Three Mile Valley and made victory possible for each one of us.

The gospel is such good news! It is an emancipation proclamation that our Great One wrote an alternate ending to our story. None of us earned it, but it is ours to fully experience.

The paradox of the gospel is death through life. Jesus turns your tomb into a womb. In other words, your sarcophagus becomes a sanctified delivery room.

The very place that declares the finality of death transforms into a place of redemptive potential through the cross of Jesus Christ.

Abundant new life emerges from abundant death. The hope we have in Jesus holds fast to the promise that whatever Jesus says should live, will live! This is part of the good that God works out through every circumstance for those who love Him.

Not only does our ever-after end well eternally, at times God advances heaven into earth and gives us an after here on earth that is full of joy.

When heaven collides with the here and now, we are in the middle of a miracle.

Our after story with Peyton is full of God's faithfulness. We regularly witness God using our story to help others walk through their valley. God preserved our family through the most intense portions of our tragic season. All of this is because God is so good.

Not only has God prepared an eternal home for you in heaven, but He's also actively bringing heaven to earth through your valley. He is the only one creative and powerful enough to author good through any and every circumstance.

As you complete your journey through The Three Mile Valley, you can know that God is working good through every step you take. Keep reading to discover my family's good-ever-after and see for yourself how God is authoring abundant life through The Three Mile Valley.

> *I consider that our present sufferings are not worth comparing with the glory that will be revealed in us.* — Romans 8:18 (NIV)

Watch "There is Always an After"
at HopeBetweenTheLines.com

CONVERSATION STARTERS

Chapter Fourteen Questions

Question: What is the difference between resolution and redemption? Can there be redemption of suffering without resolution of suffering? Why or why not?

____

____

____

____

____

____

____

____

Question: Who do you know who has experienced a beautiful "after" to their season of suffering? How does their story encourage you?

Action: Take a moment to imagine your "after." Can you see a glimpse past the valley to the glory of heaven, to greater ministry on earth, to renewal and redemption and new beginnings? Ask God to renew your hope that there will be a beautiful "after" to your story, and then hold on to that hope in the days ahead.

"The power of Jesus' death doesn't lie in
some macabre embrace of death itself,
in some dark gothic fantasy;
rather, it lies in what Jesus' followers say
his death made possible: life."

Simon P. Walker

CHAPTER FIFTEEN

The Third Mile: A Good Ever After

On November 30, 2011, our lives changed. On July 2, 2013, our lives changed again.

We were sound asleep in a camper while on a family vacation. My son, Logan, slept in the bunk above me, and Marlena was in the very narrow bed across from me. She was very pregnant—nine months' pregnant, in fact—so her sleeping in such a small and uncomfortable bed seemed like a cruel joke.

When she uttered the following words, however, I was no longer able to sleep: "I think my water just broke."

It sure had! Before anyone else at the campground was awake, we scrambled to get ourselves headed to the hospital.

First, we went to our friends' tent next door to ask if they could stay with Logan and bring him up to speed when he awoke—check. Second, to the maternity ward just five minutes away.

My nervousness was impossible to hide as I paced outside the operating room. I was covered from head to toe in blue scrubs, complete with surgical mask. The team of medical professionals calmly moved in and out of the room with the intentionality and precision of a drill team.

Every time the door opened my heart stopped. I waited. And waited. And waited.

The door opened one last time, and a nurse broke the silence, "We're ready for you."

I walked into the large operating room, fully aware of the shoe coverings that gave me sensation of gliding across the floor. I was so excited I was practically floating!

To see my wife ready to deliver our youngest child into the world brought me nearly to tears. Not yet though. Those would come later. First, the C-section.

I took my place up by her head and grabbed a seat. Apparently, some husbands don't do well with the surgical activities that play out in a C-section. Not this guy! I was fascinated by every bit of it.

The curtain stretched vertically across her shoulders, ensuring that Marlena would not be able to see what happened next. I'm not going to lie; I did peek a few times over the curtain out of sheer curiosity.

After some preliminary incisions, the doctors let us know they were getting close to retrieving our daughter. I marvel to this day at Marlena's strength throughout this whole operation. Both of us were awash in the emotion of the moment. We both had died a parent's death the evening Peyton passed.

Would this be the moment when God would resurrect our broken hearts?

The room fell suddenly silent. Every eye was focused on the middle of the operating table. The doctor triumphantly raised our newborn daughter. *Welcome to the world, Camdyn Joy Herod!*

After a brief meeting with her momma, our daughter was quickly passed off to the team of nurses who were charged with her care.

A few moments later, the nurses invited me over to the warming table. They wrapped Camdyn in a blanket and handed her to me. I could not do anything but cry as I held our beautiful gift.

My heart soared as it ached.

Camdyn didn't replace Peyton that day. She became Peyton's sister. And every day since has been full of life and loss.

This is not the happily-ever-after that we wanted. But by the grace of God, it is the good-ever-after He is authoring through our darkest days.

Does God give happily-ever-afters? I am not sure. Does He give ever-afters that are good? Most definitely.

My family has walked the temporary, sustained, secret, and tragic paths through Three Mile Valley. By the grace of God, we can live to talk about it.

Our marriage is strong. Our children pray at bedtime. Our family is committed to serving Jesus.

Our good-ever-after is full of joy.

While it is not the life we originally intended, it is the best version of the life we have now.

God has a good ever after waiting for you as well, and it starts a whole lot sooner than you may think.

CONVERSATION STARTERS

Chapter Fifteen Questions

Question: What might a good-ever-after look like in your current suffering?

____

____

____

____

____

____

____

Question: How does the thought of a good-ever-after make you feel? Does it make you feel nervous, excited, like it would be too good to be true? Why?

____

____

____

____

____

____

____

Action: Write down Bible verses about God's grace and love. Reread them whenever you have doubts about God's willingness to bring good out of your suffering.

"Once you decide that your pain isn't a barrier
to living a good life, nothing can hold you back.
In fact, moving forward and choosing life
often propels you out of your pain."

Jon Pritikin

CHAPTER SIXTEEN

The Third Mile: Your "After" Starts Now

The monarch butterfly is considered by some to be the most beautiful butterfly on the planet. Its name means "king," a definition that further illustrates its place in the butterfly family.

One time a monarch quietly landed on my knee as it took a momentary break from its flight, the distinct black, orange, and white markings on its wings utterly captivating.

Fascinated, I observed silently, until, seconds later, the butterfly lifted off in a flourish of graceful flight. It was a beautiful moment from start to finish.

That butterfly didn't always look that way, however, and it hadn't always been able to fly.

Mere weeks earlier it had been a caterpillar, limited to crawling to get around. By design, that caterpillar wove itself into a cocoon.

For ten days, everything stood still, from all outward appearances.

But we can't be deceived by what we see, because transformational activity is taking place under the surface.

The crawling caterpillar ultimately emerges as a butterfly, complete with wings for flight. God designed the monarch's journey this way, and it serves as a clear picture for us as we walk through The Three Mile Valley.

God is faithful to use everything that happens in our lives for our good. He will not waste your tears, your heartache, or your pain.

Much like the monarch butterfly's cocoon, The Three Mile Valley is a place full of transformational activity. Even through the darkness, God is working to orchestrate an after that is good for you.

The process is not something we might readily enjoy, but the product fills us with joy!

We want God to transfer us out of our pain.
God wants to transform us through our pain.

The Three Mile Valley is a place you walk through, not a place where you will stay.

The promise that you have in Christ is that there is always an after on the other side of loss, suffering, setbacks, and disappointment. You can walk through these valleys because heartache is not your home and because destruction is not your destination.

Everything you face in life has been conquered by your Savior, who will lead you victoriously through every obstacle.

God, in His infinite wisdom and grace, is using The Three Mile Valley for good. He is faithfully adding to you, even when the unfairness of life seems to only subtract from you.

Too many people fall prey to the thought that they will be fulfilled *someday*. They worship an illegitimate idol that promises a good life *over there.*

The problem with this way of thinking is that it lulls us into accepting a quality of life far below the one Jesus has purchased for us.

Jesus didn't come to give you a happy life; He came to fill you with abundant life!

The powerful reality of God's kingdom is that it exists in a perpetual state of tension. Jesus declared over and over that it was already here, but not yet arrived.

The truth is your good-ever-after starts the moment you reach up to grab Jesus' hand. As you follow Him, He faithfully brings forth unbelievably good things in impossibly difficult situations.

Yes, you will suffer, be gravely disappointed, perhaps even devastated in this life. There is no question about that. But by the grace of God, you will also abundantly live.

God's presence produces the possibility of your faith response. And your faith response leads to abundant life in Christ every day thereafter.

When Jesus enters the picture, abundant life does, too. You are no longer bound by circumstances. You are held in the grip of stronger hands.

Do not wait until you come through your Three Mile Valley to start living your good-ever-after. Reject wholeheartedly the notion that your situation has a greater say than God Himself does in your life.

Through the gospel message, He has spoken that you will live, even though you may die. His promise is sure, and His power is undeniable.

The life that lies ahead of you will be different from the life you had before you entered The Three Mile Valley. The goodness of God guarantees that your after will be eternally good, because you will encounter heaven someday. Until then, God is also working out all your pain for your good.

He is faithfully giving everything that happens in your life a divine purpose. Your best days are truly ahead of you.

Your good-ever-after has already begun! Your human mind can only imagine all God will do through The Three Mile Valley you walk. It will be worth all the sleepless nights and disappointing days!

The book of James tells of the joy we can experience by looking toward the after God is authoring through our most difficult seasons:

> *Consider it pure joy, my brothers and sisters, whenever you face trials of many kinds, because you know that the testing of your faith produces*

> *perseverance. Let perseverance finish its work so that you may be mature and complete, not lacking anything.* —James 1:2–4 (NIV)

As you walk through The Three Mile Valley and let perseverance finish its work, God adds maturity through your season of subtraction.

With poetic power, God uses the very things that pull us apart now as tools that complete us in the end. What was meant to tear you down, God uses to grow you up.

This is a good thing in another important way too, because mature followers of Jesus Christ add strength to the rest of the family of God.

I have no idea what the Lord is going to do specifically through your pain. However, I can say with all confidence that it will be good.

Watch "Your After Starts Now"
at HopeBetweenTheLines.com

CONVERSATION STARTERS

Chapter Sixteen Questions

Question: How has life subtracted from you in your current suffering? How have you seen God add to you in this season?

____

____

____

____

____

____

____

____

Question: How does a content life differ from a happy life?

____

____

____

____

____

____

____

Action: Take some time to journal a few ways you are allowing your circumstances to inhibit the life Jesus offers you. What would it look like for you to see beyond your circumstances and trust Jesus more completely?

CONCLUSION

Changing The Conversation

Words are powerful. This became painfully clear after my daughter passed away. Fresh insults have been added to injury as Marlena still wrestles with debilitating migraines to this day.

I know everyone who spoke to our losses meant well. The inconvenient truth is that not all their words landed well. Some, to be quite honest, hurt. Others confused us.

Marlena and I heard the Big Three mentioned earlier:

1.) God would never give you more than you can handle.

2.) Everything happens for a reason.

3.) Time heals everything.

True to form, these Pathological Altruisms added weight to our weary souls instead of easing our burden. The help hurt.

What if we changed the way we talk about Life and Loss? What if instead of passing around the above "Fortune Cookie Spirituality," we found something better to say? Something biblical.

I think we should try, for everyone's sake, ourselves included. Why?

The truth is better than the version we've been told.

- God would never give you more than **He** can handle.
- God **gives a purpose** to everything that happens.
- **What you do with time** can heal everything.

As I reflect on my high school cross-country race back in Duluth, Minnesota, I am amazed at the journey God has taken me on since that brisk fall day. The valley that I climbed out of to begin that race was preparation for the multiple valleys through which I would walk later in life.

The lessons of The Three Mile Valley contained in this book were also present in that long-ago race. As I ran, I learned that **now is not forever.**

Through the agony of the multiple climbs out of the valley in the physical race, I discovered that **I needed to choose wisely if I wanted to finish the race**.

And as I crossed the finish line, I experienced the truth that **there is always an after**.

No matter what life may throw at you, the Spirit of Christ inside of you is greater than the situation that surrounds you. He is your Champion who leads you in victory through every valley.

Endeavor to endure well, even to suffer well through the difficult seasons of life.

When you **think better, choose better, and watch God make it better**, you are well on your way to the life Jesus wants for you.

We should no longer be surprised by pain. Rather, we should purpose to see God's presence in our pain.

In God's good-ever-after, pain is repurposed and transformed into perseverance. What was lost is replaced with greater strength and maturity.

God alone faithfully adds to us when seasons of subtraction take away from us.

Asking "why?" is a good question, but it is not the best question. The answer to that question will never change the circumstances that first triggered your plunge into The Three Mile Valley.

And you still need to heal, regardless of what caused your pain. You still need to live, despite the challenge.

So, the most productive question in this situation becomes, "How?" And more specifically, "*How will I suffer well through The Three Mile Valley?*"

Our faith response to that question has the power to change everything. It's time to change the way we think and talk about suffering. It is a part of life, and it is packed with divine purpose.

When we hold fast to the promises of the One who is holding us, we are in the best place possible. (But notice, not the easiest or most comfortable place.)

The principles of The Three Mile Valley are simple to grasp, but they are not always easy to hold on to.

The First Mile: Now Is Not Forever

- What you see is not what you get. What you see is what you must get through.

- Perspective produces or prevents perseverance.
- Think better to live better.

The Second Mile: Cherish Your Choice

- Your response is your responsibility.
- Don't make permanent choices in temporary seasons.
- Choose better to live better.

The Third Mile: There Is Always an After

- God adds through seasons of subtraction.
- God authors good-ever-afters.
- Watch God make it better.

The path on which you are walking right now has already been conquered by Jesus. Press on and go forward with Him in victory over your valley.

You will make it through The Three Mile Valley.

You will emerge victorious.

You will make it, my friend.

Blessed is the one who perseveres under trial because, having stood the test, that person will receive the crown of life that the Lord has promised to those who love him. —James 1:12 (NIV)

CONVERSATION STARTERS

Conclusion Questions

Question: Which chapter of this book helped you the most? How did the content encourage you? Why do you think it connected with you the way it did?

____

____

____

____

____

____

____

Question: Which of the videos from this series helped you the most? What are some ways you can take what benefitted you and apply it consistently in your journey?

____

____

____

____

____

____

Action: Share one key truth that you've learned from this book and video series. It doesn't have to be in a season of suffering, necessarily.

ACKNOWLEDGMENTS

To Marlena, our journey through The Three Mile Valley is beautiful because it is ours. There is no one else I would rather walk beside.

To Logan, Peyton, and Camdyn, you are my joy.
It is a privilege to be your dad.

To my videographer, Jon Link.
Your creativity leaves me in awe.

To my on-site production lead, Wade Schroeder.
Your ingenuity and drive inspire me still.

To my video editor, Mark John Kilcoyne.
Your expertise gave this project new life.
I am forever grateful.

To my Literary Agent and editor, Cynthia Ruchti.
Thank you for investing yourself into my calling.
You are a true gift.

REFERENCES

Notes

1. Sarra L. Hedden, Joel Kennet, Rachel Lipari, Grace Medley, and Peter Tice. *Behavioral Health Trends in the United States: Results from the 2014 National Survey on Drug Use and Health. Substance Abuse and Mental Health Services Administration.* September 2015. https://www.samhsa.gov/data/sites/default/files/NSDUH-FRR1-2014/NSDUH-FRR1-2014.pdf.
2. Paul David Tripp *Dangerous Calling: Confronting the unique challenges of pastoral ministry*, Crossway (2012) P. 21
3. Muralikumar Anantharaman. *Two U.S. Pension funds see $52 mln hit from Madoff.* December 15, 2008. https://www.reuters.com/article/madoff-pension-idUSN1552227920081216

4. History.com editors. *Billionaire Conman Madoff Arrested.* December 8, 2008. https://www.history.com/this-day-in-history/billionaire-conman-bernard-madoff-arrested
5. Pallavi Gogoi and Kevin McCoy, USA Today. *Madoff investor who lost $1.4B apparently committed suicide.* December 23, 2008. https://abcnews.go.com/Business/story?id=6521133&page=1
6. Colleen P. Eren Bernie Madoff and The Crisis: The Public Trial of Capitalism. Stanford University Press P. 76
7. CNBC.com with AP. *Madoff Apologizes for Fraud Scheme.* August 3rd, 2010. https://www.cnbc.com/id/31610327

ABOUT THE AUTHOR

Dan Herod is known for starting the conversations we didn't know we needed to have. Gifted with an uncommon path in life, he writes and speaks to empower.

Born to a deaf father and surviving the aching wake of his parent's divorce prepared him for the most crushing loss a parent can meet. He knows that a soul that screams heavenward in frustration about their situation can discover how hope sometimes lives between the lines.

Dan regularly speaks about his experiences with The Three Mile Valley in churches and conferences.

Born and raised in St. Paul, Minnesota, Dan remains a Vikings fan to this day. Dan earned a BA in youth ministry and a minor in deaf culture studies from North Central University in Minneapolis, Minnesota. He is also an ordained minister. His service of over twenty years in full-time ministry has given him wonderful opportunities to serve people at the New Life (Plainfield, Wisconsin), the Christian Life Fellowship (Mayville, Wisconsin), and now as the Youth Alive director for the Wisconsin and Northern Michigan Ministries Network of the Assemblies of God.

Dan and his family reside in central Wisconsin.

Discover more at **www.hopebetweenthelines.com**

Made in USA - Kendallville, IN
26393_9798218154325
11.02.2023 1319